BKF™
Kenpo

History and Advanced Strategic Principles

By Grandmasters

Steve Muhammad and Donnie Williams

Foreword by Nijel Binns, BPG

First published in 2002 by
CFW Enterprises, Inc.

Copyright © 2002 by
Unique Publications, Inc.

DISCLAIMER

Although both Unique Publications and the author(s) of this martial arts book have taken great care to ensure the authenticity of the information and techniques contained herein, we are not responsible, in whole or in part, for any injury which may occur to the reader or readers by reading and/or following the instructions in this publication. We also do not guarantee that the techniques and illustrations described in this book will be safe and effective in a self-defense or training situation. It is understood that there exists a potential for injury when using or demonstrating the techniques herein described. It is essential that before following any of the activities, physical or otherwise, herein described, the reader or readers first should consult his or her physician for advice on whether practicing or using the techniques described in this publication could cause injury, physical or otherwise. Since the physical activities described herein could be too sophisticated in nature for the reader or readers, it is essential a physician be consulted. Also, federal, state or local laws may prohibit the use or possession of weapons described herein. A thorough examination must be made of the federal, state and local laws before the reader or readers attempts to use these weapons in a self-defense situation or otherwise. Neither Unique Publications nor the author(s) of this martial arts book guarantees the legality or the appropriateness of the techniques or weapons herein contained.

ISBN: 0-86568-218-6
Library of Congress Catalog Number: 2002012907

Distributed by:
Unique Publications
4201 Vanowen Place
Burbank, CA 91505
(800) 332-3330

First edition
05 04 03 02 01 00 99 98 97 1 3 5 7 9 10 8 6 4 2

Printed in the United States of America

Editors: Nijel Binns, BPG and Doug Jeffrey
Design: George Foon

TABLE OF CONTENTS

ACKNOWLEDGEMENTS

Foremost and above all, we thank the Divine Creator for allowing us to be of service to humanity through the study and teaching of the martial arts. We would next like to thank our immediate families for their love and support throughout the last 30 years.

From myself, Steve Muhammad, I would like to extend my appreciation to Bishop Williams for his years of friendship and support. I wish to thank my instructors Chuck Sullivan, Dan Inosanto and the late Ed Parker. I would especially like to thank my family for being so patient with me while I am on the road traveling. To my lovely wife Connie and our children Nadiyyah, Aatallah, Asaad, and Khallid, as well as Byron and Kenyetta. I love you.

From myself, Donnie Williams, I wish to thank my mother, Lissie Williams, my children Donnie Jr., Gina Floyd, Charles Contreras, Steve, Chaaz and members of The Family Church. Most of all, I thank my wife, Valerie, whom I love dearly. I would also like to thank Jerry Fieldings, Sterling Silliphant, Artie Kane, Stuart Levin, Carl Fields and Harold Borens. These individuals are special to me and were there when I needed their help most.

"We thank the Divine Creator for allowing us to be of service to humanity."

From both of us to our beloved brothers in the BKF — Jerry Smith, Ron Chapel, Cliff Stewart, Carl Armlin and Curtis Pulliam *("The Magnificent 7")* — we would like to extend our best wishes, gratitude and deepest respect for contributing the unique mix of talent, courage, dedication, integrity and legacy that became the Black Karate Federation.

We, along with the entire BKF membership, would like to thank Warner Bros. Studios, director Robert Clouse, and producers Raymond Chow, Fred

Weintraub and Paul Heller for filming the opening sequence of *"Enter The Dragon"* at the BKF's 103rd Street School in Los Angeles.

We especially wish to thank writer, historian and artist Nijel Binns, BPG, for his valuable contributions as graphic artist, technical assistant, interviewer and researcher in compiling years of material for this book.

To our BKF Family — which includes Samuel Pace, Darryl Jones, Carl Scott, Robert Temple, Earl Parker, James Jones and Diedra Decoster — thank you for your assistance in being photographed for the techniques and to Rick Wagnon for proofreading the text.

To photographers Jaimee Itagaki and Mark Campbell: thank you for your patience and wonderful work.

We would like to sincerely thank the following individuals for their interviews and access to their photographic archives. They are as follows: Leilani Parker, Ron Chapel, Al Canister, Jerry Smith, Al "Hot Dog" Harvey, Geri Simon, Brian Breye, Stu Gilliam, Samuel Pace, Dolores Sheen, Vountria Tommy Moss, Kraiguar Smith, Alvin Hilliard, Ernest Russell, Gary Goodman, Nat Moore, Richard (Ricky) Heath, Carvis Atrice Baldwin, Dan Inosanto and Chuck Sullivan.

We wish to acknowledge the dedication, vision and legacy of our late BKF brother Edward Muhammad for his sculptural and martial art accomplishments.

To our entire BKF family around the world, we would like to encourage you to stay focused so that you and those who will follow you can be assured that our tradition will continue. We wish you peace and hope that you remain dedicated to the enrichment of yourself, family, nation and humanity.

FOREWORD

The year was 1983. Donnie Williams and Steve Muhammad asked me to assist them in compiling their first martial arts instructional book. The writing and publication of that book represented the nation's first international martial arts book written by African-American masters. As it turns out, *"Championship Kenpo,"* which was published by Ohara Publications, Inc., became a bestseller and landmark publication for the Black Karate Federation.

In the years that followed, *"Championship Kenpo"* has proven to be a personal milestone for me as a writer. It blessed me with the opportunity to become more closely associated with these two gentlemen whose legendary accomplishments I am still discovering … decades later.

During the research for *"Championship Kenpo,"* I quickly realized that there was so much more to Steve Muhammad, Donnie Williams and the history of the BKF. To my dismay, I knew even then that I would not be able to cover everything in that one publication. I realized that the complete story and remarkable history of the Black Karate Federation was not written back then, and to be quite honest, could not be completely recorded at this time either. Although I began work on this project, with the full intentions of learning as much as I possibly could about masters Steve and Donnie, their art, the BKF and its history, little did I know how monumental this undertaking would prove to be. I've attempted to chronicle 30 odd years of material in a short space of time. In the process, I have recovered the legacies of hundreds of people whose lives have been touched by the BKF. Needless to say, the BKF story will be the subject of books, documentary and feature films well into the future.

I am humbled to have the honor of being a contributor to this current publication and to have the privilege of mining the depths and presenting the treasures of this dynamic period in American martial arts history. This was a time when men such as Steve Muhammad and Donnie Williams figured prominently on the martial arts scene. Together — with their contemporaries such as Chuck Norris, Bruce Lee, Joe Lewis, Byong Yu and many, many others — they wove a colorful tapestry whose brilliance has not diminished with time. These early years of martial arts history in America were written during an era of great social change that included the rise of the Civil Rights movement and a growing consciousness among African-Americans.

Without a doubt, the Black Karate Federation has emerged through its infancy to become an established, global institution whose history and achievements shine brightly as a beacon across the landscape of our nation. To the great men and women of the BKF and to grandmasters Steve and Donnie, I salute your achievements.

— Nijel Binns, BPG

ABOUT THE AUTHORS

Steve Muhammad

Grandmaster Steve Muhammad is a co-founder of the Black Karate Federation and the organization's first president. He is also one of the most dynamic and celebrated figures in the history of American martial arts. From his days as a tournament competitor with an unrivaled championship record, to becoming a trainer of fighting champions and of thousands of martial art practitioners worldwide, Steve Muhammad exemplifies the true spirit of the martial arts tradition. In short, he is a warrior and a true gentleman.

Born in Topeka, Kansas in 1944, Muhammad was the youngest of several siblings, all of whom were raised in a tight knit and fairly athletic family. Muhammad's first exposure to the fighting arts actually began observing his mother! To keep her boys in line, she developed "a mean right hook."

In high school, Muhammad became an outstanding athlete who excelled in football, baseball and track. He later attended Kansas State University on a football scholarship before leaving to join the Marine Corps. While in the military as a member of the Pathfinders, he received his first real exposure to the martial arts. Training with the Pathfinders was similar to training with the Green Berets — it was

ABOUT THE AUTHORS

intense and highly disciplined.

During his military years, Muhammad was stationed at Camp Pendleton, which is in Southern California. Twice a week he drove north to Los Angeles to train in kenpo with Ed Parker. Even after he was later transferred to El Toro Marine Base, he continued to travel and train in Los Angeles. Muhammad's training was eventually interrupted with a tour of duty in Vietnam. The experience of fighting in Vietnam gave him discipline and a first-hand look at the reality and brutal effectiveness of combat.

After his enlistment was over in 1963, Muhammad returned to California and immersed himself in the study of kenpo with Ed Parker. He earned his first black belt three years later under Parker's instructors Dan Inosanto and Chuck Sullivan.

As a tournament competitor, Muhammad became a member of the West Coast Karate Team. During those early days of sport karate, he faced renowned fighters such as Joe Lewis, Al Dacascos, Chuck Norris and Benny Urquidez. Many tournament veterans called Muhammad "The fastest hands in karate." He later received the ultimate tribute from the late Bruce Lee, who said Muhammad had the "fastest hands I had ever seen."

In the decades following Muhammad's magnificent tournament career, he became interested in developing a more personal approach to fighting and began to introduce his own techniques in his training. Some of his theories, such as "Brain Sight" and the "Principles of Mathematical Fighting" have revolutionized his art.

Muhammad had "the fastest hands I had ever seen."

The quiet-spoken Muhammad has twice been awarded the Golden Fist Award by his colleagues, and he has been nominated for the *Black Belt* magazine Hall of Fame for his outstanding contributions to the martial arts. He is co-author of *"Championship Kenpo, The God Side of Kenpo"* and *"Brain Sight."*

Mr. Muhammad has also found time to appear in a few films. His most notable role was in *"Enter the Dragon."* In this classic Bruce Lee movie, Muhammad played the role of Jim Kelly's instructor. Additionally, Mr. Muhammad has worked with actor Wesley Snipes for several years as his bodyguard and accompanied him throughout his film career.

Donnie Williams

Grandmaster Donnie Williams was born in 1947 in Savannah, Georgia. His early upbringing in the ghetto gave him a keen instinct for survival, which he channeled into his martial arts training to become one of the most dynamic and outspoken personalities in sport karate. By the time he retired from competition, Williams had amassed more than 85 championship trophies and began to appear in several motion pictures, including *"Truck Turner," "Black Belt Jones"* and most notably *"Enter The Dragon."*

Donnie Williams began his martial arts training in Texas with a brief introduction to the *shotokan* karate system under *sensei* Jerry Atkins. Shortly thereafter, he enlisted in the U.S. Navy. His four-year tour took him to Korea, where he received his first exposure to *taekwondo*. Williams immersed himself in training and continued his studies after returning to the states. Settling in California, he began training in that Korean art with master Byong Yu.

Four years later, he had developed into a superb kicker who gained renown on the tournament scene for his aggressive fighting style, as well as unique ring antics. It was this combination of fun and fury that earned Williams the nickname "Clown Prince of Karate."

ABOUT THE AUTHORS

It was during this time of tournament competition that Donnie Williams met Steve Muhammad. During the ensuing 14 years, Williams learned about Muhammad's deceptive kenpo techniques.

As a co-founder of the Black Karate Federation, along with Steve Muhammad and the other visionary African-American martial artists of his time, Donnie Williams was particularly instrumental in molding an organization that would represent, train and support black martial artists and tournament competitors nationwide. His outspoken, yet firm and friendly approach — combined with the quiet leadership of Steve Muhammad — helped to carve a trail that hundreds of inner city youth would follow for decades to come.

As a born leader and entrepreneur, Donnie Williams has been the pioneer and catalyst for every significant milestone for the BKF, such as the negotiations that led to the publication of "*Championship Kenpo*," for which he is co-author, the wildly successful "*BKF Magazine*," "*The God Side of Kenpo*" and this publication.

As his experiences with the life-changing benefits of martial arts study became more apparent, Donnie Williams began to more vigorously pursue his spiritual calling. This has led to what Williams acknowledges as his most significant achievement. Today, Donnie Williams is more often referred to as Bishop Williams since becoming an ordained Bishop of a non-denominal congregation in Southern California known as The Family Church. As a minister and spiritual guide, Bishop Williams infuses every sermon with his full life's experience as a warrior, leader, media personality and teacher.

ABOUT THE AUTHORS

Nijel Binns, BPG

Nijel Binns is an English-born writer of philosophy, theater and the martial arts. As a professional writer, his first international work was contributing to *"Championship Kenpo."* That was 1983. In 1990, Binns wrote and published, *"Nuba Wrestling™: The Original Art."* This treatise explores the ancient martial arts of Kemet (Egypt) and is largely responsible for a re-examination of the origins of the martial arts.

In 1998, Binns presented his findings on the Arts and Entertainment television documentary, *"The Martial Arts,"* which actor George Takei narrated. Binns' research material was requested for inclusion as part of a college course offered by Scholargy, Inc. in Temple, Arizona in 2001. As a leading authority on 12th Dynasty martial arts in Kemet, Binns, a member of the Association for the Study of Classical African Civilization (ASCAC), frequently travels throughout the country presenting lectures on the subject.

As an internationally renowned artist and head of the fine art sculpting firm, Nijart International, Binns is a master sculptor and craftsman of bronze, monumental and life-sized statues. His 16-foot "Mother of Humanity™" bronze monument is a Los Angeles landmark.

Binns' sculptures have been commissioned by The Los Angeles Urban League, Fox Studios, Sony, The Great Blacks In Wax and other organizations. Known as "sculptor to the stars," Binns' masterworks are owned by Michael Jackson, Stevie Wonder, Natalie Cole, Jackie Chan, Nelson Mandela, Denzel Washington, Celia Cruz and a growing list of luminaries.

Nijel Binns has been a practitioner of the martial arts since 1968 and has been featured in many articles in *Inside-Kung-Fu* and *Black Belt* magazines. Binns is also a member of the Screen Actor's Guild and has worked closely as stuntman, stunt coordinator and actor under the tutelage of *"Enter The Dragon"* director Robert Clouse in the films *"The Big Brawl," "Force Five"* and *"China O'Brien" I* and *II.* Binns has also worked with veteran stunt coordinators Pat Johnson and Terry Leonard on *"Karate Kid II"* and *"Imposter,"* which starred Gary Sinese.

The 16-foot tall Mother of Humanity™ monument by Nijel Binns, BPG.

INTRODUCTION

From the time the Asian systems of combat were introduced to the shores of the United States of America, the involvement and influence of the African-American martial arts has been evident from Coast to Coast. This is especially true from the end of World War II to today. There has been a long, distinguished but unheralded list of great African-American martial artists and teachers, including grandmasters Moses Powell, Ronald Duncan, George Cofield, Mfundishi Maasi and Thomas LaPuppet. All of them loomed large on this new American frontier.

Other, more controversial figures, such as master Karieem AbdAllah, blazed new trails. In November 1967, against all convention and to the consternation of the martial arts establishment, he boldly proclaimed his belief that the martial arts were indigenous to black culture. Although lacking the benefit of the wealth of data that is available today, Karieem held firm to his convictions and set about "creating" a highly effective system of karate he called the KA System. It was a system that was built around the culture of the black man in America.

In California, also during the 1960s, martial artist, competitor and teacher Steve (Sanders) Muhammad was undergoing a similar evolution through the mastery of his art ... kenpo. As Muhammad began racking up tournament success after success, he introduced a flow and distinct African rhythm patterns to the already modified kenpo that grandmaster Ed Parker had taught him.

The organization he co-founded, the Black Karate Federation, assembled an eclectic mix of martial arts talent, including co-founders Donnie Williams, Jerry Smith, Cliff Stewart, Ron Chapel, Karl Armelin and Curtis Pulliam. They have enriched the field of martial arts and sport karate in America by producing outstanding fighters and model citizens who would define an age. Their teachings have produced leaders on two continents: Africa and America. These leaders, in turn, have themselves become teachers and leaders of men and women of all cultures and ethnic groups.

"BKF Kenpo: History and Advanced Strategic Principles" presents this legacy through the teachings of grandmasters Muhammad and Williams. It uncovers an often overlooked chapter in world history and the history of the martial arts in America. It redefines what it means to be an individual, regardless of ethnic background, a martial artist regardless of system, a master, and leader in this bold, new time in our nation's history.

CHAPTER 1

THE HISTORY & EVOLUTION OF BKF KENPO

Knowledge is the foundation

upon which all strategic

principles are built.

Thereforc, Advanced Strategic

Principle No. 1 is ...

You must study.

All expressions of human activity are products of their time. When it comes to combat, it is no different. The development of the art and science of combat, which we call martial arts, has also been influenced by time, the environment and countless other variables. As this information relates to strategic thinking, which is the focus of this book, when we discuss the art and science of kenpo within the Black Karate Federation (BKF), the reader will find that without a knowledge and history of the events that preceded this book, it is impossible to understand the present or to be prepared for what is yet to come. After all, is not the real purpose of strategy to plan in preparation for success? It is with this in mind that we will now examine the events of the past.

Most practitioners would agree that the martial arts are an activity that involves interaction between human beings for the purpose of self-development and/or self-protection. To fully appreciate how this activity has evolved into a science, we must go back to acknowledge the emergence of the human species on this planet.

At this time, the oldest known hominid remains are more than four million years old and were discovered in the Afar region of northeastern Ethiopia, Africa. Named "Lucy" by her discoverers and "Dinkenesh" by the Ethiopians, in the scientific community she is known as *Australopithecus afarensis*. Research has shown that her DNA has populated the entire planet. Since the emergence of *Australopithecus afarensis*, the single, most overriding desire of the human species has been the need for survival. To that end, a wide variety of strategies for survival have been devised throughout the millions of years since the arrival of Lucy. These strategies range through the ages from simple rock throwing and hitting with sticks, to incredible, multi-dimensional psychic battles that take place in an unseen spiritual realm. In this book, we will examine strategies that relate to physical combat, mental development and spiritual growth.

If we begin our studies with China, Okinawa, Japan or Korea, we will find that the history of the martial arts has been relatively well documented since the 16th century. However, in the Occident, an awareness and study of the martial arts occurred rather recently as U.S. servicemen, who were exposed to Asian cultures overseas, returned home after World War II (1941-1945). One of the earliest references to the martial arts was made in a 1941 U.S. publication, *National Geographic* magazine.

As a travel magazine noted for covering global cultures and traditions, an article titled "*Daily Life in Ancient Egypt*" appeared in this particular issue. The article included illustrations of dozens of African martial arts practitioners from a location named "Beni Hasan," which translates as "hill of the sons of Hasan." Those illustration were only 25 percent of the complete contents depicted on the walls of a rock tomb belonging to Prince Baqet III of the 11th Dynasty in Egypt *(Figure 1)*. His tomb was one in a series of 39 rock tombs hewn in cliffs along the banks of the Nile. They are found at a location known during the time of the ancient Egyptians as "Mahez." This describes a long-horned African antelope.

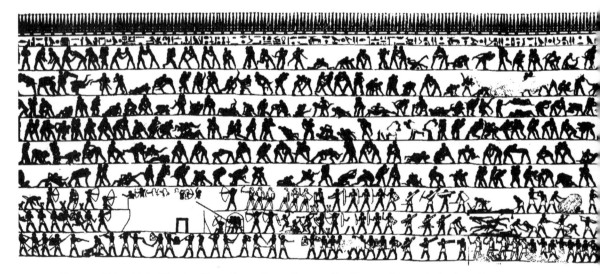

Figure #1 - This illustration, found on the wall of a rock tomb belonging to Prince Baqet III at Beni Hasan in Kemet (Egypt), dates to around 2,800 B.C. These and many other records have been known since antiquity and grandmasters Mas Oyama and Ed Parker referred to them in their first books on the martial arts. *Courtesy of Nijart International*

Mahez is located in an area approximately midway between the city of Cairo in the north and the famous Temple of Luxor in the south. What is of great significance to our study here is that the illustrations on these rock tombs represent the oldest known examples of martial arts practice in the world.

In Asia, although the history of the martial arts are more readily accessible to the martial arts practitioner and historian, it is a history that goes back to a certain point in time and does not take into account the emergence of the human species on the continent of Africa or the methods of self-defense that had developed there. Yet, as all modern human beings did originate in Africa, how can a study of this history be ignored? Up until now, the most popular and frequently cited accounts of the origins of the martial arts refer back to the exploits of the Indian priest Bodhiharma, who upon arriving in China in the 6th century, subsequently founded the Shaolin Temple martial arts. Now, rather than simply retelling this story as countless books, magazines and web sites tend to do, we will study this history in greater detail and go back even further in time to reveal the identity of Bodhiharma's guru, a man by the name of Siddhartha Guatama, commonly referred to as the Buddha or *"The Enlightened One."*

THE PATH OF WISDOM

We need to fully understand his background to understand his path of wisdom, which became known as Buddhism, a cornerstone in the development of kenpo and other martial arts. We will also discover the connections to the much older Beni Hasan tomb paintings and the references that were made to them by name, by two renowned 20th century masters of the Asian martial arts such as Ed Parker and Masutatsu Oyama.

Masutatsu Oyama (1923-1994) was the acclaimed *kyokushinkai* founder and martial arts grandmaster who was born in South Korea. He began studying *shotokan* with Giko Funakoshi, the second son of master Gichin Funakoshi, who introduced karate to Japan from Okinawa. He also studied *goju-ryu* from Mr. Neichu So.

Figure #2 - In 1958 Masutatsu Oyama, "The Godhand" (left), wrote his first book *"What Is Karate?"* He stated in print and pictures that Africa is the birthplace of the martial arts. Compare Oyama's stance to this ancient Egyptian from 2,800 B.C. *Courtesy of Nijart International*

Mas, as he was called, was well known for his incredible feats of strength and endurance. His acclaim reached near mythic proportions when, in order to demonstrate the true power and effectiveness of karate, he fought and killed bulls with his bare hands. Mas Oyama was given the nickname "The Godhand" by his contemporaries and worked tirelessly to spread the philosophy of karate throughout Asia and the world.

In 1958, Mas Oyama published his first book, "*What is Karate,*" which was the same year the American civil rights leader Dr. Martin Luther King, Jr., published his first book, "*Stride Toward Freedom: The Montgomery Story.*" If these two events are viewed side-by-side during this era, any suggestion regarding Africa as the birthplace of the martial arts would not have been a welcomed idea. It certainly would not have prompted anyone's research or study. Yet in this one, rare and classic book, Mas Oyama actually wrote that, "The oldest records we have concerns unarmed combat on hieroglyphics from the Egyptian pyramids..."

Mas Oyama specifically mentions the location as "Bein Hasan" (Oyama's spelling). From this short but pregnant reference, it suggests that somewhere, at some time, these findings were the subject of detailed study. There were some inaccuracies in Mas Oyama's references (the paintings were in "rock tombs" and not Egyptian pyramids and the name "Bein" should have read "Beni"). In the reprinted edition to his second book, "*This is Karate,*" published in 1972, Mas Oyama corrects the spelling to "Beni Hassan" and briefly recounts the reference to Africa from his first book.

In addition to acknowledging publically that Africa was the birthplace of the martial arts, which would be akin to declaring in 16th century Italy that Jesus Christ was a man of color, Mas Oyama is actually photographed in a *gi* (training uniform). In this photo, he is in a stance that "links" his beloved martial art to Africa. Two photographs appear in the introductory pages of both "*What is Karate*" and the reprinted follow-up book, "*This is Karate.*" Mas Oyama *(Figure 2)* is standing in a salutary and spiritual stance that was well-known throughout ancient Kemet (the correct term for Egypt). In Oyama's stance, his left foot is forward and both hands are raised, with the palms facing out. Some people believe (not necessarily Oyama) that this stance is interpreted to mean, "I have no weapons." On the surface, this is a shallow and simplistic explanation. In the tradition of ancient Kemet to which Oyama openly refers, placing the left foot forward was symbolic of truthfulness. It meant that a person should walk with the intent of the heart (which is on the left side of the body) and go forward with righteousness to stamp out falsehood and evil. It is interesting to note that modern day military cadence emphasizes "*left*-right-*left*" in its drills. The left foot is also symbolic of the left side of the brain, which receives from the pineal gland, the creative impulse. The hands represent an extension of the heart. They are influenced by the quality of one's heart. In showing our hands, we show our heart. This is the ancient African tradition and proper meaning of the stance as it is practiced today.

Although Mas Oyama stands lightly on the ball of the left foot with the knee bent, as opposed to having both feet flat, the caption below this picture in "*What is Karate*" further reinforces an African tradition. The text acknowledges the spiritual thought that this gesture meant to Mas Oyama and to all of karate. Mas Oyama states that what is even more vital to karate than strength or technique is "spirit." In this short statement, he gives repeated references to Zen ("Ch'an" in Chinese) Buddhism, which as we know, entered China and later Japan, from India.

We will pursue this reference to Buddhism made by Oyama. Before we do so, however, it is interesting to point out that this same salutary gesture was not only used in ancient Africa, but is still used in many parts of Africa today. The Zulus, for example, greet high masters by placing the left foot forward and raising both hands, palms facing forward. Located in Southern Africa, the amaZulu or "people of heaven," live in KwaZulu Natal, an area bordered by the sea, the Drakensberg, Mozambique and the Eastern Cape. Zulus claim their descendants are from the people in ancient Kemet in the north. So, when master Mas Oyama, in word and deed taught that karate belonged to the world, he was quite correct, but he also gave credit to its source. Grandmaster Oyama was a true pioneer and noble master who worked throughout his life to show how the martial arts could be used to uplift and unite humanity.

FATHER OF AMERICAN KARATE

In the United States of America, karate received its start with the visionary efforts of kenpo grandmaster Edmund Kealoha Parker (1931-1990). Universally acknowledged as the "Father of American Karate," Parker was responsible for, among many things, introducing the phenomenal martial arts master Bruce Lee to the world during the 1st International Karate Championships held in Long Beach, California in 1964.

As a trailblazer and innovator in the field of martial arts, Parker was also a prolific writer who authored a series of books. His first book was *"Kenpo Karate - Law of the Fist and the Empty Hand,"* which was published in 1960. In that book, Parker credits Africa as the birthplace of his martial art. Mr. Parker wrote that, "...records seem to link KENPO KARATE (Mr. Parker's emphasis) even back to the time of the Egyptian Empire." According to Dr. Ron Chapel, who is one of Ed Parker's early students and a highly skilled kenpo practitioner, Mr. Parker was aware of the African origins of the martial arts, even though he never focused on this during his teachings.

In 1990, historian and martial artist NiJel Binns, BPG wrote and self-published a research booklet titled *"Nuba Wrestling™: The Original Art."* Mr. Binns began his research into the highly-detailed, four-volume books

Edmund Kealoha Parker

titled *"Beni Hasan,"* which were written by English Egyptologist Percy E. Newberry in 1893. Mr. Binns undertook seven years of critical analysis and interpretation of this body of work, as well as

Figure #3 - Black Buddhist monks from India and Chinese monks trained together in the early days of Shaolin. Dozens of monks are depicted on two 12-foot long mural paintings in the White Garment Hall at the Shaolin Temple in Honan, China. *Courtesy of Nijart International*

investigating material from Jean F. Champollion, Hippolito Rosellini, John G. Wilkinson and Richard Lepsius, who were all European explorers in Kemet during the 17th and 18th centuries. Binns published his findings, which concluded that the Nuba of Sudan, Africa practiced a form of martial arts well more than 2,800 years before Christ. This system of martial arts, which included weapons as well as fortification and certainly empty hand self-defense, formed the oldest and most complete martial arts methods ever recorded in antiquity. The practice of these arts existed before the founding of Egypt and was based on what later became identified as Kemetic philosophy, which blossomed in 12th Dynasty Kemet. The wisdom of ancient Kemetic masters spread from Africa and influenced the world. Mr. Binns has provided hard facts and proof of the statements that were only briefly referred to by masters Mas Oyama and Ed Parker. They did not elaborate on these statements for political, cultural or other reasons.

Even prior to Mr. Binns' research, there were in fact, many references in Asia that provided connections to the martial arts influence from Africa, but these too were never explained, and only referred to in passing. For example, a visitor to China today will find two monumental, 12-foot long mural paintings on the walls of the White Garment Hall in the Shaolin Monastery in the Honan province of China (Shaolin, or "Young Forest" in the Mandarin dialect is "Sil Lum" in Cantonese Chinese and "Shorinji" in Japanese). These two murals are well-known and feature dozens of Chinese and obviously black Shaolin monks engaged in boxing training together *(Figure 3)*. Not surprisingly, because no one has come forward to present the complete history of how and why these black people appear in these paintings, this history has largely been ignored. Owing much to ignorance, some people will say the figures represent "dark Chinese" monks. Many martial artists in the West will look at these paintings and simply will not see black people — period. This attitude is not surprising and recalls to mind how Hollywood approached the popular 1970s television series *"Kung-Fu,"* which gave America its first look at the Asian martial arts. Producers bypassed the Asian martial arts genius Bruce Lee for whom the lead role was specifically written and instead cast a Caucasian actor, David Carradine, to play his part.

The history of the dark skinned brothers of the Chinese Shaolin monks have been conspicuously excluded all together from the history of the martial arts. Owing to the "impropa-ganda" and stereotyping of African people during and after slavery, various cultures are not quick to embrace the African and are even less inclined to teach the African what many believe he should already know. Rather than engage in speculation as to who these dark skinned people are, or weave elusive stories about "bronzed monks," we need only look to the impartial sciences of anthropology and genetics for the facts.

In 1998, the Proceedings of the National Academy of Science concluded a study by the Chinese Human Genome Diversity Project and made public their findings, which stated that, "Most of the population of modern China — one-fifth of all the people living today — owes its genetic origins to Africa ..." The study was the result of a consortium of several leading research groups in the People's Republic of China, in combination with the Human Genetics Center at the University of Texas Health Science Center in Houston, Texas. The National Natural Science Foundation of China funded the research.

In addition to genetic evidence linking China to Africa, archeological evidence has recorded close to 100 "pyramids" that are located in a 100 kilometer area around the city Xi'an in central China. This site is also well-known as the location of the famous life-size terracotta warriors. Further study of the history and art of the Shang and Chou dynasties in China will reveal even more African influences. All of this is not to say, however, that Chinese culture is African. It is not and should never be misinterpreted to be. Instead, this information and evidence points to a clear interaction and anthropological connection that must be acknowledged if the complete story is to be told in its entirety.

As it relates to the murals mentioned earlier, the sciences of genetics and anthropology provide further insight into the accounts of the martial arts in China, specifically pertaining to the master of the famous Buddhist priest from India, Bodhiharma. Known as "Ta Mo" in China and "Daramu" in Japan, Bodhiharma was a 28th generation disciple of Siddhartha Guatama, otherwise known as the Buddha. Bodhiharma traveled to China where he taught his brand of exercises. This became the foundation for Quan fa or "Chuan fa," which means "The way of the fist." In Japan, it corresponds to their word "kenpo," which means "The law of the fist" or "Fist law."

The history of Bodhiharma and his influence in China has become legendary, but the more profound story of his master, Siddhartha Guatama, and the philosophy of Buddhism is rarely — if ever — discussed when explaining the history of the martial arts. It is vital to our understanding of kenpo and the martial arts that we look closer at India, the times in which Buddha lived and who the Buddha was. This will help us to clarify Mas Oyama's references to Africa in his words and pictures, as well as provide the full story for the black Buddhist monks who appear on the murals at the Shaolin Temple in China today.

TRUE HISTORY OF BUDDHA

As a matter of record, the true history of the Buddha from India has been known to most serious scholars for many generations. For example, one of the most brilliant and exhaustive studies to look at languages and histories of nations are the books *"Anacalypsis, An Attempt to Draw Aside the Veil of The Saitic Isis"* and *"An Inquiry into the Origin of Languages, Nations, and Religions, Vol. 1 and 2."* They were written after years of research by English historian and linguist Godfrey Higgins, Esq.

He published this massive two-volume work in 1833. In it, he gives many references to the Buddha such as, "...he is continually described as a Negro, not only with a black complexion, in which he agrees with Cristna ("Krishna" – a name that means "the Black one" – ed.), but with woolly hair and flat face."

Figure #4 - Contrary to the popular image of Buddha today, early statues and paintings from the 4th century B.C depict Siddhartha Guatama (*The Buddha*) as a black man. Gautama developed a path of enlightenment, later referred to as Buddhism, which was a philosophy of liberation to help his people resist the slave ideology of northern invaders. *Courtesy of Nijart International*

Higgins further states that, "In the most ancient temples scattered throughout Asia, where his worship is yet continued, he is found black as jet, with the flat face, thick lips and curly hair of the Negro." These references accurately describe the earliest depictions of the Buddha. It is only centuries later, when Buddhism gets introduced *outside* of India, that the Buddha takes on the Chinese, Japanese, Korean and other Asian features that we associate with him at present. However, for the record, let it be known that Buddha, the first and original Buddha, was black *(Figure 4)*.

A study of the history of India will reveal that at one time, all of India was occupied by two distinct negroid types. One had a dark complexion with a flat nose and curly hair, often described as "nappy" or "pepper-corn" hair. The other was also dark complexioned but with an somewhat aquiline nose and straight hair. These black people were architects of the glorious Indus Valley civilization and its culture called Harappan, which was named after one of the two great cities, Mohenjo-Daro and Harappa, built around 3,000 B.C. in southern India. Those cities were the culmination of smaller towns which date back to 6,000 B.C.

Around 1,500 B.C., a wave of invaders from the northern hemisphere flooded into India. These invaders adopted the word "Aryan," which is an ancient Sanskrit term meaning "noble one." This is the term that Adolph Hitler, the German dictator from World War II, used in the 20th century as part of his misguided "master race" ideology. Aryan, or "aryan brotherhood," is also a term used by quite a few white supremists today. In ancient India, these invaders began a slow, methodical and systematic destruction of the Indus Valley civilization. Their strategy was to first assimilate the local religions and deities of the native people. Next, they gradually instituted a multi-level, color-based, caste system they called Brahminism. This system placed the invading Caucasian minority on the top (they called themselves "brahmin" or "priestly ruling class") and the majority of darker people whom they conquered on the bottom (the "sudrahs", or "working class"). Records of the Aryan invasions into India are aptly preserved in Indian literature such as the "*Rig Veda*." More recently, a scientific article appeared in the *San Francisco Chronicle*, on May, 26, 1999, confirming this history through the use of genetics. Researchers from the University of Utah and Andhra Pradesh University in India confirmed — through a study of DNA and the Y male chromosomes of the Indian population — that there were a group of males with European affinities who were largely responsible for this invasion 3,000 or 4,000 years ago.

Although this strategy for enslavement is similar to most patterns of racism seen around the world, the slavery and color based separation into castes that the Aryans introduced into India is unique. This ideology was skillfully blended with indigenous beliefs to form a religion and a way of life that eventually became known as Hinduism. Its Brahmin priesthood were successful in keeping the caste structure in place. Even today, the once intricate and liberating African philosophy of karma and rebirth, that are now a part of Hinduism, have been strategically reworked and used to suggest to millions of people that if they were born into slavery, it is their karma or fate. This was the world that the dark skinned Siddhartha Guatama was born into. He searched in earnest for a way to bring light to his people and end this suffering. Out of his own enlightenment, a philosophy was born that became known as Buddhism. This revolutionary philosophy offered a path towards liberation from mental and psychological slavery for millions of black and brown people. Buddhism offered a path of salvation and the end of the concept of being born and re-born into slavery.

Godfrey Higgins wrote in 1833 that, "Between the Brahmans and the Buddhists there exists the greatest conceivable enmity. They (the Brahmans) will hold no communication with them, believing themselves to be made unclean, and to require purification, should they step within even the shadow of a Buddhist."

Today, at this hour, an underclass called "Untouchables" still exists in India after hundreds of years. They are poor blacks who are on the lowest rung of the caste ladder system. An Untouchable is subject "by law" to having his tongue cut if he dare read any sacred scriptures. He can be beaten or even killed if his shadow is allowed to fall on a Brahmin. He may be required to wear a broom tied to his back so as to sweep away his footsteps as he walks. He must look down, and never make eye contact, with a Brahmin. The women are frequently raped and their men murdered at the whim of a Brahmin, often without any legal consequence. Today, this is sanctioned by law. Many Untouchables who are conscious of the history of their country turn to Buddhism as a way to escape the caste ideology as countless generations before them have done. To these early rebels, Siddhartha Guatama, the black, curly-haired Buddha was their liberator.

Eventually, the Brahman succeeded in overcoming the Buddhists in India. They used the same strategy to lay claim to the Buddhist religion, while at the same time destroying their temples and pushing the original adherents out of India. It was around 260 B.C. that many Buddhists were forced to flee to Thailand, Vietnam, China, Tibet and neighboring countries throughout Asia. The history of these black holy men throughout Asia explains the affinity experienced by the 20th century African American soldier who fought in South East Asia during the Vietnam War.

The point here is that generations who struggled under physical, mental and spiritual slavery in India are the reason why images of the black freedom fighter Buddha, as well as black Buddhist monks, show up all throughout Asia and China, where Buddha's disciple Bodhiharma was to visit many years later. This then, is the untold history of Buddha, his times and his path towards liberation known as Zen or Ch'an Buddhism. This is the history of the philosophy that has so profoundly influenced the practice and development of the martial arts in Asia and around the world.

There is an interesting cosmic circle that has formed with the history of Buddha and the practice of kenpo in America. Black people struggled against oppression in ancient India, which resulted in a martial art and philosophy that were transmitted to China and Japan as kenpo. This was then transmitted to America and adopted by black people who were struggling against oppression in the United States.

The history of the African holocaust in the so-called "new world" is recent history. Africans continue the job of reversing the debilitating effects of this event which has caused amnesia and cultural memory loss regarding their rich heritage, while their oppressors siphon off their genius to build empires around the world. From the impact of slavery as it relates to the martial arts, little information was available concerning the African origins of the martial arts and the great mental, physical and spiritual powers that the practice of the martial arts could produce. In fact, for a time in America during the late 1950s and early 1960s, many Caucasian pioneers in the field openly expressed racist sentiments by saying that they believed blacks did not have the mental capacity to perform the martial arts. The origin and true history of the martial arts were unknown to blacks "and" whites of that generation in much the same way as how the original legacy of Buddha is unknown even to the majority of black Untouchables who are still enslaved in India today. Given the history and origin of kenpo as a martial art coming from black India, and further back to Africa, the history and legacy of kenpo within the Black Karate Federation places it as the direct — and most legitimate descendant — of a magnificent and most ancient martial tradition.

So, as the history of the martial arts goes, we will now continue with the more frequently quoted account of Bodhiharma finding the Buddhist monks at Shaolin in China. As the legend goes, Bodhiharma found the monks lacking the physical and mental stamina needed to perform even the most basic meditation practices, so he corrected this by teaching them moving exercises designed to both enhance chi flow and build strength. From the onset, an internal (soft) and external (hard) component of the martial arts were taught to the monks. The exercises he introduced to the monks formed the foundation for the development of contemporary Chinese martial arts and the incredibly prolific variations that exist today.

EVOLUTION OF KENPO

At various stages, the evolution of the modern martial arts have moved from China into Okinawa, Japan and Korea. As kenpo was transmitted into Japan, one of the styles, or versions were refined by the Mitose family and became known as *kosho-ryu kenpo*. Dr. James

Mitose (1915-1981) was sent from Hawaii to Japan at the age of five to study the Mitose family tradition of Ch'uan Fa at the Mt. Akenkai Kosho-Shorei (Old Pine Tree) temple. After returning to Hawaii, grandmaster Mitose taught and awarded black belts to to the following six students: Giro Nakamura, Thomas Young, Paul Yamaguchi, Arthur Keawe, Edward Lowe and William K.S. Chow.

William K.S. Chow (1914-1987) was also trained in Chinese Shaolin Ch'uan Fa under the guidance of his father Hoon Chow, who was a Buddhist Priest from Shanghai, China. Hoon Chow immigrated to Hawaii just prior to the Boxer Rebellion of 1900. The Boxers were a secret society, known as the Fists of Righteous Harmony that attracted thousands of followers for the purpose of expelling Europeans, whom they referred to as "foreign devils" from China. Hoon Chow moved to Hawaii and continued to practice the Shaolin Ch'uan Fa of Southeastern China (Kwangtung and Fukien). This is the style he taught his son, William K.S. Chow. Master William Chow incorporated many of the things his father had taught him into what he would be the first to term "Kenpo Karate."

William K.S. Chow, who was five feet one, was raised in Hawaii, in a culture in which size, strength and street fighting ability were highly regarded. He began to alter Shaolin Ch'uan Fa to fit his own body mechanics. Chow made kenpo faster, more powerful and more readily suited towards modern street-fighting situations. In the process, he began a transformation of the art by adding linear movement, joint locks and takedowns to the circular movements of chuan fa. He also focused on striking vital points and nerve centers on the body. William K.S. Chow's Hawaiian Kenpo system, which he called kara-ho kenpo, was innovative for its time because it was an amalgamation of several disciplines.

Edmund Parker (1931-1990) was a first generation student of William K.S. Chow. Mr. Parker brought kenpo from Hawaii to the continental United States in 1954 and modified it even further. In her 1997 book, "*Memories of Ed Parker*," Mrs. Leilani Parker quoted her husband as saying, "Professor Chow explained the need for modifications and additions in the art. Chow did not teach me many of the modifications and developments I later came up with, but he started me looking for other avenues. Chow gave me the first 15 to 20 percent of my knowledge in the martial arts and the rest was my own."

Ed Parker introduced Steve Sanders Muhammad to kenpo, and he also trained under Chuck Sullivan. Both of these men encouraged him to develop his expression of the kenpo system, just as Parker and William K.S. Chow did before him.

For the past three decades, kenpo in the BKF (sometimes referred to as BKF Kenpo) has been an art and science defined primarily by the innovations of Steve Sanders Muhammad with the assistance of students such as Vountrai Moss and Kraiguar Smith. The martial art of the Black Karate Federation has evolved from its initial conception and today, most of the founding members — with the exception of Steve Muhammad and Donnie Williams – have branched off to create other organizations and expressions of the martial arts. However, like jazz music, the uniquely American inclination to evolve and transform has resulted in kenpo, as practiced within the BKF, becoming a living, dynamic and vibrant martial art.

Figure #5 - Steve Sanders (right) as a white belt with his instructor, Dan Inosanto (center), and Bob Cook (left) at Salt Lake City, Utah, after a successful tournament. *Courtesy of Dan Inosanto*

Guro Dan Inosanto was a first generation student of, and instructor for Ed Parker's kenpo system and Bruce Lee's Jeet Kune Do system. As Steve's first instructor in kenpo in 1964, Dan recalls that, "Steve was, without a doubt, the fastest hands I had ever seen in the kenpo system, bar none. He had speed singularly and in combination."

Muhammad would earn his brown belt under Guro Dan but was, as a white belt, already garnishing his share of tournament trophies *(Figure 5)* that showed the effectiveness at which he applied his art.

Figure #6 - Steve Sanders training with his instructor Chuck Sullivan, under whom he earned his first-degree black belt in 1966.

Courtesy of Chuck Sullivan

Steve Muhammad's own evolution beyond the American kenpo that he was taught by Ed Parker and Dan Inosanto actually began with a visit to Mr. Parker's Santa Monica school. It was during this training session that he became aware of Chuck Sullivan, an American kenpo instructor, and Ed Parker's business partner.

Sullivan recalls that, "Steve was one of the most amazing students I ever taught. He would make any instructor look good. He took whatever you showed him and did it just a little better."

Muhammad was equally impressed by Mr. Sullivan who, being similar to himself in size and build, made that art work in ways he had not seen before. Recalls Muhammad, "When I saw Chuck Sullivan, I saw that he was a small man like I was. When he moved, he had perfect form. I transferred to his school where he allowed me to do the techniques the natural way my body would move."

Muhammad began with Dan Inosanto in 1964 as a white belt and continued until he received his first-degree black belt under Chuck Sullivan in 1966. According to Ed Parker, Muhammad was a

Figure #7 - In Hawaii, Steve Sanders scores with a perfect side kick to the chin of David Krieger. He won this match and more than 300 additional trophies in the years that followed. *Courtesy of Steve Muhammad*

unique student.

"Students like Steve master not only physical speed, but mental and perceptual speed as well," said Parker.

Chuck Sullivan calls Muhammad "the quintessential counter-fighter" *(Figures 6,7,8).*

Steve Muhammad, as a tournament competitor and teacher, believed that his art was designed for self-defense purposes first. In the "asphalt battlefields" of South Central Los Angeles throughout the turbulent 1960s, the techniques were frequently put to the test in real-life situations. This became the catalyst for the need to develop a realistic approach to kenpo. It forced the art to move beyond theory and to application. Muhammad will be the first to

Figure #8 - In this rare photograph from 1967, Steve Sanders (top right) is a member of Ed Parker's Kenpo Karate team competing in Hawaii. Competing and winning overseas earned both Steve Sanders, and American kenpo, international recognition.   *Courtesy of Alvin Hilliard*

tell you that he never taught tournament fighting per se.

"It is the intense training in the basics and the emphasis on facing the reality of the nature of real street fighting that made our tournament fighters superior," he says.

Fighters incorporated Mr. Muhammad's signature use of timing, broken rhythm, speed and techniques, which allowed them to engage in each and every competition with intensity as if it were a life-or-death confrontation. Often times, when their opponent would be going for "points" or swinging wildly — without control or technique in full-contact fighting — BKF kenpo students showed that they were technicians who could execute moves with explosive power, speed and precision. This is because their art was designed for street application and not tournaments. With this understanding, early competitors and technicians such as Donnie Williams, Vountria Moss, Jr., Kraiguar Smith, Al Harvey, Michael Baptist, Willie Shelmire, Terry Beal, Lawrence Gordon, Ronald Hill, Samuel Pace, Carl Scott, Gary "Rabbit" Goodman, Lenny Ferguson and many, many others dominated tournament karate in several divisions throughout various periods in the history of the BKF. They found themselves, as young men often in their teens, facing older, more seasoned tournament fighters. They would go on to win many regional and world championships, while changing the face of tournament karate forever *(Figure 9)*.

STILL EVOLVING

Kenpo in the BKF is still evolving and being taught along the same principles upon which it was developed. For example, in combat and sparring drills, safety equipment and the excessive padding that was popular during the 1970s are not encouraged. Kenpo is an art of self-defense — not a sport. It was not designed for use with safety gear and many kenpo techniques such as eye gouges, finger thrusts and clawing techniques are neutralized by using it. Perhaps even more importantly, students who use safety gear are not conditioned properly in training and are not accustomed to the reality of being hit. In today's environment, the average young adult is bigger and stronger; therefore, facing an opponent while wearing safety gear is unrealistic.

In the ring, or on the street, BKF kenpo continues to develop warriors, while encouraging new members of all ethnic groups to walk the path of peace. They not only learn to

STEVE SANDERS

ERIC AUSBORN
CARVIS (WILDMAN) BALDWIN
ERIC BERDETT
AARON BLUNT
REGGIE BOWDEN
JOE BROWN
NATHAN CRIUSE
LENNY FERGUSON
AL (HOT DOG) HARVEY
RICKIE HEATH
STANLEY HICKMAN
MICHAEL HOLMES
JAMES HONEST
VICKIE JOHNSON
ANDY KROBE
RODNEY LOCKHART
VONTRIA MOSS
SAM PACE
DONALD RAY
RON ROBINSON SR.
RON ROBINSON JR.
CARL SCOTT
KRIAGUER SMITH
JOE SWIFT
ROLAND TALTON
TED TAYLOR°
ROBERT TEMPLE
DONNIE WILLIAMS
FRANK WILSON
JEROME WOODS
JEFFREY WRIGHT

Figure # 9 - This excerpt from Ed Parker's Kenpo Karate Family Tree lists most of the first generation students produced by Steve Sanders. A few of the names are misspelled, and others such as Billy Allen, Ronnie Sanders, John Townes and Albert Walker were not recorded.

Courtesy of Ricky Heath

become great fighters, but they learn through the art of combat how to develop those mental skills and spiritual attributes that make them champions in life.

A BRIEF HISTORY OF THE BLACK KARATE FEDERATION

If you look at the 1960s, you will see that it was a time of sharp contrasts in America. During this generation, "baby-boomers" spoke a language of peace, love and soul. In 1960, music pioneer Berry Gordy started the Motown Records label. BKF members would later provide security for many of the leading Motown legends of the day. In 1961, optimism was high with the inauguration of President John F. Kennedy. By 1962, the U.S. commitment in Vietnam deepened. By 1963, civil rights leader Medgar Evers and President Kennedy were both assassinated. The riots in Watts, California followed in 1965.

In 1967, The Beatles pleaded that, "*All You Need is Love*," but that year Newark, N.J. erupted in three days of riots. President Lyndon B. Johnson appointed Illinois Gov. Otto Kerner to head a commission to study the disturbances. The Kerner Commission stated that, despite some political rights for blacks from the civil rights movement, unemployment, ingrained racism and poor housing still remained. The commission concluded that: "Our nation is moving towards two societies: one black, one white — separate and unequal."

By 1968, the "dream" was crumbling as Martin Luther King Jr. and Senator Robert Kennedy were both assassinated. As America moved even deeper into Vietnam, Muhammad Ali — world heavyweight boxing champion, icon and hero to millions — had his title stripped and was willing to face jail rather than be drafted to fight an unjust war.

On March 4, 1968, one month before the assassination of Dr. Martin Luther King, Jr., J. Edgar Hoover, the head of the Federal Bureau of Investigation (FBI), sent a communique to field operatives. It specifically identified the Nation of Islam and its founder, the Honorable Elijah Muhammad, as well as Dr. Martin Luther King Jr.'s Southern Christian Leadership Conference (SNCC), as primary

Figure #10 - The decade of the 1960s was a time of turbulence and sharp contrasts, yet Steve Sanders and Donnie Williams, seen here in 1971, remained committed to civil rights and fair treatment for blacks in the martial arts.

Courtesy of Donnie Williams

targets of Hoover's Counterintelligence Program (COINTELPRO). This operation was the FBI's secret program to undermine a growing black consciousness that was sweeping the country during the 1960s *(Figure 10)*. COINTELPRO was finally exposed to the public in March, 1971, when secret files were removed from an FBI office and released to the news media.

The most serious of the FBI's strategies for disruption within the black community were those directed at "Black Nationalists" between 1966 and 1971. These programs were supposed to "expose, disrupt, misdirect, discredit, or otherwise neutralize the activities of black nationalist, hate-type organizations and groupings, their leadership, spokesmen, membership and supporters."

Figure #11 - In 1967, Steve Sanders (above) taught free classes at Manchester Park in Los Angeles. Many inner city youth could not even afford uniforms at that time. Steve Nelson (center, extending a right front kick) and Greg Massengale became Steve Sanders' first students, pre-BKF.

Courtesy of Alvin Hilliard

Figure #12 - Samuel Pace (left), William McLauren, Bonnie Brooks (seated) and Archie Grissom were some of Donnie Williams' first students. This shot was taken in 1969 at Duarte High School.

Courtesy of Alvin Hilliard

Agents were instructed to "inspire action in instances where circumstances warrant." The most intense operations were directed against The Black Panther Party for Self-Defense. Founded by Huey P. Newton, Bobby Seale and later led by Eldridge Cleaver, the organization was started in 1967 in Oakland, California to patrol black neighborhoods and monitor routine police mistreatment of blacks.

By the mid-1960s, the influence of men such as Dr. King, who had developed a mass following on the basis of appeals for "equal rights," was being rapidly supplanted by younger leaders such as SNCC's Stokely Carmichael and H. Rap Brown, who espoused a much more proactive vision of black empowerment.

These events of the past should not be lost to current practitioners of BKF Kenpo because when several black men met in Los Angeles to form an organization in 1969, the cause for which they fought was much in the spirit of the times. As athletes, the founders of the BKF experienced racism in the martial arts and wanted to gain a stronger and more unified voice in sport karate events. These days are a far cry away from the days (1966) when one popular white southern champion openly declared that he did not "want to compete with niggers." There were times when tournament promoters would intentionally match black competitors against each other and employ other tactics to eliminate black participation. Finally, these pioneering young men who dared to speak up were ostracized and labeled "militants" in the hopes of further discouraging their participation in the martial arts. All of this would continue unabated until the arrival of The Black Karate Federation.

MEETING IN L.A.

In the late 1960s, young black martial artists in their mid 20s had been meeting for some time and training at various locations in and near Los Angeles, such as the Teen Post, Manual Arts High School, the West L.A. Karate Institute, Duarte High School and Manchester Park *(Figures 11,12,13,14)*. The group included Steve Sanders, Ron Chapel and Curtis Pulliam, who trained in kenpo; Cliff Stewart (originally from the *goju* system) had trained in *hapkido*; Jerry Smith *(shorin-ryu)*, Donnie Williams *(taekwondo)* and Frenchie

Figure #13 - Ron Chapel (far right) with his first martial arts class at Manual Arts High School in the 1960s in Los Angeles.

Courtesy of Ron Chapel

Humble, *lima lama*. Mr. Humble was later killed in Germany in a car accident. There was also Isiah Williams, Curtis Faust (now Abdul Muhammad), who trained in lima lama, as well as Lloyd Francis, a *tang soo do* stylist from San Diego, Charles Murphy with the five animal system gung-fu, Jim Kelly with Okinawa-Te (he taught at Vernon Avenue and Broadway in Los Angeles), Bob Owens with *shotokan* (Owens died in a fatal auto mechanic shop incident) and Hugh Van Putnam, a hapkido practitioner. The group meetings coalesced at Van Ness Park, where every Saturday, dozens of black men would come together, train and

Figure #14 - Cliff Stewart (age 19), as well as Jerry Smith, held frequent classes for the neighborhood youth during their early college years.

Courtesy of Ron Chapel

Figure #15 - Fifth-degree shotokan sensei William Short prepares to execute a breaking technique. At a Compton College demonstration in 1967 (top right), the progressive sensei Short wore African attire. Former student Richard "Ricky" Heath (lower right) came to the BKF and went on to a notable career in the music industry, law enforcement and the ministry.

Courtesy of Ricky Heath

exchange techniques.

Another significant martial arts figure in Los Angeles during this period was William Short. At an imposing 6-foot, 4-inch, 278 pounds, "Willie" Short became one of the first African-American to earn a black belt in shotokan karate overseas, which he did in 1953. Short studied shotokan with Kobayashi *sensei* while stationed in the Air Force at Tachikawa AFB, Japan *(Figure 15)*.

Upon returning to the United States, Short opened the Kobayashi School of Karate at 8711 So. Western Ave. in Los Angeles, before moving to 9108 So. Western Ave. According to Brian Breye (Willie Short's senior belt), Short was not embraced by the white martial art community. Many schools that had white owners did not even accept black students at that time. However, Short, who spoke fluent Japanese, was well-known to the Japanese community. They invited him to perform in Little Tokyo during their Nisei Week Festival in the summer of 1960 *(Figure 16)*.

Figure #16 - In this 1967 photo taken at the Los Angeles Trade Tech College, Brian Breye, from the Kobayashi Karate School, is shown in a demonstration match with Steve Sanders. Chuck Norris (seated, left) judges as Tino Tulasega (co-founder of the Lima Lama system) referees.
Courtesy of Ricky Heath

As an elder, 20 years the senior of Steve Sanders, the soft-spoken Short was ahead of his time. In college, he majored in African-American history and made two trips to Ghana, Africa (1970 and 1973). He returned to the states and began to wear traditional African garb at demonstrations. As a close friend of Dr. Ron Karenga, creator of the Kwanzaa holiday and a progressive black man, he taught his students about Africa and African-American history.

"Willie" Short was a close friend of Dr. Ron Karenga, creator of the Kwanzaa holiday.

Student Al Canister recalls some of those moments.

"Sensei Bill Short introduced us to Japanese masters Mas Oyama, Morihei Ueishiba, and Gogen Yamaguchi when we went with him on a six-week trip to Japan in 1969," recalls Canister. "He taught us about Malcolm X, the Honorable Elijah Muhammad, bean pie and whiting fish. He was a diverse and international figure."

Sensei Bill Short's evolving consciousness regarding his African heritage, however, could not supersede his staunch devotion to his traditional Japanese upbringing in shotokan. It was not easy for him to see beyond the confines of styles and systems and thereby permit him to expand on the idea of solidarity among African-Americans in Los Angeles. That job would fall to a younger, more relaxed generation that also loved their cultural roots but were able to embrace the martial arts, regardless of style.

Consequently, the dynamic energy created in this eclectic mix resulted in several of Willie Short's younger students being attracted to the BKF. Former students Ernest Russell, Gary "Crusader Rabbit" Goodman, Eddie "Iron Man" Horton, Ricky Heath and Al Canister, who remained with sensei Short, would soon combine Short's emphasis on conditioning and hard shotokan style basic training with the techniques and advanced fighting principles learned from the newly emerging group, in general, and the kenpo of Steve Sanders, in particular. It is in this same spirit in which Bruce Lee would evolve his *jeet kune do* concepts. All of these pioneering young men were totally dedicated to the martial arts, and the rich and fertile environment they created set the stage for the successful tournament records of many later BKF legends.

Cross-training in various styles would give students, participants and competitors a knowledge of karate, hapkido, tang soo do, kung-fu and several additional disciplines.

As a reflection of the times, the push for a united voice in sport karate was soon taken up in earnest. Black martial artists were tired of being cheated so often at tournaments. If it was not because of race, it was because of bias towards a particular style or system. Perhaps the decisive factor was the infamous 1969 tournament between Joe Lewis and Steve Sanders. Everyone, including Joe Lewis, acknowledged that Sanders was cheated out of a win. All of these elements brought about an awareness for the need of a new strategy. They reasoned that if they united together, they could stand as one. Cliff Stewart, Ron Chapel and Jerry Smith soon met with the intent of establishing an organization for blacks in the martial arts. It would further motivate the group to see how Asians were representing themselves with organizations such as the Japanese Karate Association (JKA) and the Chinese Martial Arts Association.

THE MAGNIFICENT SEVEN

The regular Saturday meetings at Van Ness Park attracted dozens of other martial artists and soon a core group began to form. Calling themselves "The Magnificent Seven" after the popular Japanese Samurai film by Akira Kurosawa, the group included Cliff Stewart, Jerry Smith, Ron Chapel, Steve Sanders, Donnie Williams, Karl Armelin and Curtis Pulliam. Smith recalls the group.

"We were the right mix of people at the right time," he says. "We created a great and unbeatable mix of techniques."

Steve Sanders was the catalyst for these Saturday workouts, and therefore became the unofficial leader of a team who, like the group in the film, was comprised of several distinct, colorful and sometimes clashing personalities.

At a follow-up meeting, several names for an organization were suggested. Jerry Smith, whose background was in graphic design, created a few logos with the initials "BKF," which stood for the Black Karate Federation. During the meeting, several logo designs were introduced to the group.

Evolution of the BKF Patch from the top: (a) Besides the fist as a symbol of black pride in the 1960s, Willie Short's concept of a "Brotherhood" Karate Federation provided some inspiration for (b) the designs by Jerry Smith of the dragon, cobra, red, black and green flag drawing, and (c) the politically charged "power to the people" concepts. (d) There was a "Wo Ying Chuan" patch that was short-lived before a return to (e) the popular "Kenpo Karate" patch, which was the standard BKF patch for many years. *Courtesy of Ron Chapel and Brian Breye*

The organizational structure of the BKF formed with Steve Sanders, the most prominent and visible member of the group. Therefore, he was unanimously selected to be the organization's first president. Jerry Smith became the first vice-president, Cliff Stewart the secretary, Ron Chapel the technical historian and Karl Armelin was treasurer. From this core group, which included Donnie Williams and Curtis Pulliam, the Black Karate Federation was officially founded.

During this period in 1969, the group of pioneers were young men in their 20s who were highly influenced by the times. No one could have predicted that in the decades to come, their efforts would spawn leaders in the fields of law, medicine, motion pictures and sports. In an era of high hopes, dismal failures, government attempts at sabotage, the rise of Los Angeles street gangs and the desperate need for heroes within the black community, the BKF provided a way for talented, young black girls and boys in South Central Los Angeles to achieve their fullest potential. Generations of children to come, of all backgrounds, stand to benefit from the continuing evolution of this truly American expression of an ancient African martial arts tradition.

What the early pioneers of the BKF may have lacked in experience, they made up for in enthusiasm and dedication to a cause. Admittedly, there were some who did not fare well in this process of turbulence, change and evolution. By far, however, the lives of thousands of inner city youth — of all ethnic groups — have been enriched forever.

In 1969, a short time after its inception, the BKF began to more actively support and train black fighters in the increasingly visible world of sport karate. Sports in America have provided tremendous opportunities for many professional athletes in modern times such as golf's Tiger Woods, basketball's Michael Jordan, and Venus and Serena Williams in tennis.

For blacks in the martial arts in the 1970s, they saw the potential to forge a new chapter in the American dream. Many BKF fighters would go on to win numerous titles and championships in spite of the challenges and prejudices they faced. Al "Hot Dog" Harvey, noted researcher and first generation BKF student explained that, "We were being groomed in the Jackie Robinson and Arthur Ashe school of martial arts in terms of behavior and how to professionally conduct and represent ourselves. As far as talent was concerned, what we saw Michael Jordan do on a basketball court, we had several athletes like him in the BKF whom we got to see and train with every night."

"We were kids, fighting grown men, and beating them!"

Alvin Hilliard, also a first generation BKF student who later became one of the first kickboxing champions remarked, "We were kids, fighting grown men, and beating them! We didn't know at the time how ground-breaking the achievements we were making actually were."

THE SHEENWAY SCHOOL

Although it was unofficial, the Sheenway School, which we will soon look at, provided one of the first training locations for the BKF. The first official Black Karate Federation school opened in late 1970-71 at 10302 So. Western Ave. in Los Angeles *(Figures 17,18,19)*. Known as "The 103rd Street School," it was the home of the original students of the BKF, which included Ronnie Sanders (Steve's brother); Vountria Tommy Moss, Jr. (the first superstar for the BKF); Frank "Nitty" Wilson, a Crenshaw High school track star who was dubbed "the fastest human alive" *(Figure 20)*; Ronald Hill; Kraiguar Smith; Samuel Pace; Al "Hot Dog" Harvey; Carl Scott and BKF photographer Carvis "Wildman" Baldwin *(Figure 21)*.

The 103rd Street school was the home of champions and future champions. In those days of fanatical dedication, if the windows did not fog up during a workout, it was not considered a workout... period. Martial arts champions such as Joe Lewis, Cecil Peoples and Benny Urquidez frequented the school to train because they always knew they could get a good workout there. Lewis would come there to prepare for his tournament battles.

The 103rd Street School achieved notoriety as the location chosen to film a portion of the immortal martial arts film, *"Enter The Dragon,"* which starred Bruce Lee. Released by Warner Bros.

Figure #17 - The famous 103rd Street School at 10302 South Western Ave. in Los Angeles was home to many champions in the BKF from 1969 to 1971. If the windows did not fog up, you did not have a good workout.

Courtesy of Capt. Wildman

Figure #18 - Along with Bonnie Brooks, John Henderson, (right) from Ed Parker's Kenpo school, became one of the first Caucasian members in the Black Karate Federation. Vountria Moss, Reggie Bowden, Billy Allen, Gerald Mays and Jerry Davis are to Henderson's left.

Courtesy of Capt. Wildman

Figure #19 - From left: Nathan Cruise, Samuel Pace, Billy Allen and Reggie Bowden at the 103rd Street School.

Courtesy of Capt. Wildman

Figure #20 - The BKF's legendary and unbelievably quick Frank "Nitty" Wilson (above). Dubbed "The fastest human alive," he executes a perfect flying side kick to Ronald Hill's head. As a native of Chicago, Frank was said to have trained under the infamous John Keehan, who was also known as Counte Dante. Frank later moved to Los Angeles.

Courtesy of Alvin Hilliard

Figure #21 - Carvis Atrice Baldwin (right – "Captain Wildman") built an unforgettable persona as an outgoing, charismatic performer and competitor whom insiders believe provided the inspiration for the character "Sho Nuff," played by actor Julius Carry III in the hit Motown film, *The Last Dragon.*

Courtesy of Alvin Hilliard

Figure #22 - In this memorable scene from the classic Bruce Lee film *"Enter the Dragon,"* Jim Kelly, who plays "Williams," says good-bye to his instructor, played by BKF co-founder and president Steve Sanders. Legend has it that director Robert Clouse, as well as Bruce Lee, wanted Steve Sanders for the role that Kelly eventually landed. *Courtesy of Alvin Hilliard*

Studios in 1973, the film contains a scene in which Jim Kelly ("Williams") goes into the karate school to say good-bye to his instructor (Steve Sanders) *(Figure 22)* and the assistant instructor (Donnie Williams).

Some believe that the film's director, Robert Clouse, and the star, Bruce Lee, originally had Sanders in mind for the role that Kelly eventually got. Kelly, by the way, would use that film to launch a successful, but all-too brief film career during the "blaxploitation" period of the 1970s.

In the *"Enter the Dragon"* scene, BKF co-founder Jerry Smith, as well as several BKF students, can be identified. As fate would have it, those few seconds of exposure in *"Enter the Dragon"* has cemented the continuing legacy of the BKF because of Bruce Lee and the global impact that the film continues to have.

Even as history was being made with feature films and world-class black and white martial arts competitors who trained at the 103rd Street School, the BKF still suffered its share of harassment from local law enforcement. In the film *"Enter the Dragon,"* Williams leaves the karate school and two policemen stop him in an alley. For blacks at that time, and in many instances still today, this event is a familiar occurence. In the early days, the entire BKF school would jog in formation throughout the neighborhood while chanting cadence. From the dojo, they would run north to Sportsman Park (now Jesse Owens Park) at the corner of Central and Western Avenue. On one particular occasion, while more than 100 students and their families trained at the park, police helicopters circled overhead and squad cars converged on the park. In another instance, there were reports of strange, unidentified people who would drive up to the school and take pictures through the windows. However, none of this deterred the BKF from performing its service to the community: keeping youth out of gangs and away from drugs.

In fact, nowhere in the history of the BKF can anyone show that BKF students advocated violence or that they were some sort of left or right wing paramilitary group as some would have preferred the public to believe. Keep in mind how COINTELPRO targeted "any" group or organization who sought to raise black consciousness and help black youth feel better about themselves. It mattered not that five out of seven of the BKF founding members were Vietnam veterans, four of whom later became public servants in law enforcement, and one, a spiritual leader of a church. These were the events that shaped the Black Karate Federation.

A short while after the 103rd Street School was established, an official branch of the BKF was developed at the Sheenway Kindergarten Culture Center, located at 10101 Broadway in Los Angeles *(Figures 23,24,25,26,27,28)*. Dr. Herbert A. Sheen founded this and his daughter, Dolores "Dee" Sheen, later became the executive director. She and her son, Erin Blunt, (co-star in *"The Bad News Bears," "Car Wash"* and other films between 1976 and 1978), became students in BKF Kenpo.

Figure #23-24 - The Sheenway School, founded by Dr. Herbert Sheen in Los Angeles, added kenpo to its curriculum in 1971 and helped to groom many BKF students for success.

Courtesy of Sheenway Museum Archives

Figure #25 - First generation BKF student Al "Hot Dog" Harvey being promoted to sixth-degree black belt in 1982 by Steve Sanders at the Sheenway School. Martial artist and musician, Ted Taylor ("Baron of the Blues") looks on. The late Taylor's music (insert) is still a best seller in Europe.
Courtesy of Sheenway Museum Archives

Figure #26 - Robert Temple (right) grew up in the BKF and became an instructor for a whole new generation.
Courtesy of Sheenway Museum Archives

Figure #27 - Steve Sanders trains a young Carl Scott, who would later become a pioneer and film star in Hong Kong kung-fu films ("*Soul Brothers of Kung-fu,*" "*The Dragon Lives,*" *etc.*). Students Nathan Cruise, Rod and Ron Robinson, Jr., (left), as well as Kraiguar Smith (far right), Erin Blunt and two others look on.
Courtesy of Sheenway Museum Archives

Figure #28 - Dr. Herbert A. Sheen, M.D., receives an honorary black belt from Steve Sanders in 1975 for years of outstanding work in the service of his community. A great warrior, Dr. Sheen passed away one year later.
Courtesy of Sheenway Museum Archives

Dee Sheen expanded the Sheenway program in 1971 to include the martial arts. Steve Muhammad has named Dolores "The Mother of the BKF" *(Figure 29)*. Assistant BKF instructors such as Alvin Hilliard and his brother Melvin "Sugar Bear" Hilliard (aka "The Fighting Hilliards") were sent to Sheenway from the 103rd Street School to work with the beginners. They would eventually help to produce champion BKF students such as the irrepressible Terri

Figure #29 - Dolores Sheen, whom Steve Muhammad refers to as "The Mother of the BKF," continued in the tradition of her father. For three decades, she was the matriarch for several generations of inner city students and kenpo practitioners at Sheenway.

Courtesy of Sheenway Museum Archives

Figure #30 - The first BKF full-contact fighters (clockwise from bottom) John Townes, Samuel Pace, Gary "Rabbit" Goodman, Kraiguar Smith and Ernest Russell. Jerry Smith (center, boxing shoes) was their trainer.

Courtesy of Samuel Pace

Dent, Lenny Ferguson (the first African-American to win International Grand Championship in 1975) and Robert Temple, who developed as a talented teacher and competitor. The Sheenway school provided valuable awareness of and commitment to community service. Hundreds of boys and girls have had their lives transformed through the martial arts at Sheenway under the direction of Steve "Papa" Sanders *(Figure 30, 31, 32, 33)*.

Figure #31 - "The Fighting Hilliards" of the BKF, Alvin and Melvin ("Sugar Bear") Hilliard, trained and fought with an indomitable spirit. "Weasel,"as Alvin was called, worked with Bill Cosby (lower right) doing character voices for his "Fat Albert" cartoon television series.

Courtesy of Alvin Hilliard

Figure #32 - The BKF frequently took part in community events such as this Watts Festival Parade along Central Ave. in 1979.

Courtesy of Sheenway Museum Archives

Figure #33 - Steve Sanders, known simply as "Steve" to many and "Papa" to most, was the father figure to several generations of boys and girls from the inner city.

Courtesy of Sheenway Museum Archives

THE SECOND SCHOOL

The second official BKF school opened in 1971 at 4273 Crenshaw Blvd. in Los Angeles. Gino Barbre, an artist and local businessman at a nearby auto dealer *(Figure 34)*, financed the school. Under the leadership of Steve Sanders, the Crenshaw school became home to BKF champions such as Alvin Prouder, who held four world titles at the same time and surpassed Joe Lewis by winning the coveted Internationals title four times. His sister, Cynthia Prouder, also excelled in competition and later became a professional boxer *(Figures 35, 36, 37)*.

Figure #34 - Gino Barbre (right), artist and businessman, is seen here with BKF student "Chicken" Gabriel at the 1973 Internationals. Barbre provided the capital to open the second BKF school at 4273 Crenshaw Blvd. later that year. *Courtesy of Carvis Atrice Baldwin*

The Crenshaw school was also home to actor/comedian Stu Gilliam, veteran of more than 21 film and television shows since 1968 and one of the oldest BKF members to earn his black belt. Stu became the official griot or historian for the BKF. Around this time, martial artist Jim Kelly, the International middleweight champion in 1971, opened one of three school a few doors away from the Crenshaw School. Soon however, his commitment to a motion picture career took the bulk of his time *(Figure 38)*. Kelly went on to star in numerous films such as *"Black Belt Jones," "Hot Potato," "Three the Hard Way"* and *"Golden Needles."* Nat Moore and Hap Halloway, who became a sponsor of tournament fighters such as Alvin Prouder, later purchased his schools.

In 1991, Robert Temple and Robert Humphrey opened a BKF school at 10953 South Broadway. That school became established a few years later and Amen Rahh, formerly known as Andre Young *(Figure 39)*, was in charge. With his emphasis on African history and culture, Amen Rahh later relocated to Africa where he opened the first international BKF school in Kenya, Africa in January of 1997.

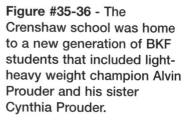

Figure #35-36 - The Crenshaw school was home to a new generation of BKF students that included light-heavy weight champion Alvin Prouder and his sister Cynthia Prouder.

Courtesy of Sheenway Museum Archives

In all of the BKF schools, particularly in the early years, the military style discipline and training that the students received — combined with inner city determination and tough street smarts — forged a powerful statement of unity. In the group's first appearance, the Lima Lama tournament in 1971, 150 students walked into the event in single file, with military precision and all carrying... briefcases. Each briefcase contained a fighter's "armor," which was their starched and folded karate gi. They wanted people to know they were there to take care of business. Because the group presented a strict, no-nonsense image, the announcer introduced them as the "Black Panther" Karate Federation. Interestingly enough, The Black Panther Party for Self-Defense, although they were not affiliated with the Black Karate Federation, became aware of the BKF around 1971 through students Alvin and Melvin, whose uncle David Hilliard (author of *"This Side of Glory"* with Louis Cole), was Huey P. Newton's close associate. However, the BKF was never conscripted into the Black Panther Party, nor any other organization for that matter. They were a family unto themselves whose

Figure #37 - Throughout the 1970s and into the 1980s, master Steve Sanders continued to train and produce champions for the BKF at the Crenshaw school. *Courtesy of SMCM Enterprises*

only concern was to excel in the martial arts. Nonetheless, even in the absence of any political affiliation or aspiration, in later years some BKF founding members, not surprisingly, did reveal that they were aware of the presence of the FBI, which had begun to monitor their activities. The founders spoke of wire taps, while younger students recounted experiences with police surveillance, frequent stops and questioning.

Figure #38 - While Jim Kelly (left) watches, Charlie Crawford narrates the action during a 1971 demonstration in which a blindfolded Hugh McDonald slices a watermelon on the stomach of Kelly's student, Ray "Blue Steel" Davis. Kelly operated a few schools in the Crenshaw district before a growing film career took most of his time.
Courtesy of Sheenway Museum Archives

Figure #39 - BKF instructor Amen Rahh (top left) emphasized the study of African culture and founded the first international branch of the BKF in Kenya, Africa in January 1997. *Courtesy of Samuel Pace*

It was also during this time of dynamic social activity and growing consciousness within the black community in South Central Los Angeles that the antithesis of these good works would find expression with a 15-year-old youth by the name of Raymond Washington. Other local gangs encouraged he and a few of his friends (Stanley "Tookie" Williams and Jamiel Barnes) to start their own gang, which they called the "Baby Avenues." Later, they changed the name to the "Avenue Cribs" and finally the "Crips." Today, there are Crips gangs across the country and variations in several countries.

For the record, there were a number of street gangs already in existence in Los Angeles before the Crips. However, during these times, there were new, clandestine forces at work that were set in motion to drag black youth into the type of gun violence that characterized this new generation of gangs, such as the Crips and their rivals, the Bloods. Eventually, Tookie Williams was sent to prison and has been on Death Row in San Quentin, California for the 1979 murder of four people.

Thousands of lives have been adversely affected since the founding of the Crips in 1969. Interestingly enough, that was the same year that the Black Karate Federation was formed. As previously mentioned, four out of seven BKF founding members were Vietnam veterans. After the military, many of them continued to serve their community and country without recognition. Yet, in an ironic twist of fate, to the surprise and bewilderment of many, Tookie Williams, the founder of the Crips, actually received a nomination from a member of the Swiss legislature for a *2001 Nobel Peace Prize*. It was reported that Wiliams was nominated for his efforts to change his life. He had also authored a series of books about his gang experiences, in the hopes of discouraging youth from the lifestyle he helped to create.

Tookie Williams is remembered within the BKF for brief encounters they had at the now defunct Rio Theater on Imperial and Western avenues in Los Angeles. On occasion, the BKF was hired to provide security for the theater. However, in an attempt to turn the lives of these youth around, Williams and Barnes actually participated in an Upward Bound Program under the direction of a BKF founding member. As time went on, more gang members, hoping to distance themselves from what was quite literally a dead end life-style, actually joined the BKF family and began to train in kenpo under "Papa" Sanders. With former gang members in their midst, this also attracted local law enforcement to the school. Not surprisingly, later findings seem to indicate that covert COINTELPRO type tactics may have been used to infiltrate the BKF school and sow dissension among its ranks.

Despite these setbacks, the BKF remained committed to helping inner city youth and providing a way to improve their lives. Many well-known celebrities such as Richard Pryor *(Figure 40)* joined with Mable King, Dolores Sheen and Donnie Williams at Sheenway. On one occasion, they offered $92,500 to a program that was designed to bring about a gang truce from the destructive

Figure #40 - From the left, actress Mable King, Dolores Sheen and Donnie Williams stand with Richard Pryor at Sheenway. The actor/comedian donated $92,500 for programs to keep kids out of gangs and off drugs. *Courtesy of Sheenway Museum Archives*

activities that have claimed the lives of thousands of youth in the community. Sanders would often teach children for free if their parents were unable to pay, simply to get them off the streets. Many BKF students went on to become doctors, lawyers and professionals in many diverse fields. Today, they acknowledge a debt of gratitude to grandmasters Sanders and Williams and the entire BKF family that cannot be measured, nor repaid.

While maintaining their service to the community during the early 1970s, the BKF also worked diligently toward their primary goal: the representation within the young world of American sport karate. With a unified voice, the organization quickly gained respect and paved the way for a more balanced representation of all races that we see today. Although at this time, many black martial artists were successfully competing, Steve Sanders became a figurehead for blacks in karate in much the same way as Jackie Robinson did in baseball. His phenomenal abilities, leadership and quiet strength had an enormous impact on the American youth, who had never had a black fighting figure to emulate. With his brief appearance in *"Enter the Dragon"* and due in part to the success of the Jim Kelly films that followed, black youth gravitated to Sanders as a larger-than-life tournament champion, folk hero and symbol of a fighter in a decade in which black people were conscious of, and fighting for, their rights *(Figure 41)*.

Figure #41 - Like Jackie Robinson in baseball, Steve Sanders became a larger-than-life tournament champion, folk hero and symbol of justice for all competitors in the martial arts. *Courtesy of Sheenway Museum Archives*

HUGE IMPACT

The results of the pioneering and diplomatic efforts of the BKF in those early days made them a dominant force in the world of karate. There were major events in the earlier years such as the March 22-23, 1975 Sheenway Tournament at the Hollywood Palladium with master Ted Tabura and Cecil Peoples and the 1976 U.S. Tournament of Champions sponsored by actor/director Eric Laneuville at the L.A. Sports Arena. That event attracted celebrities such as The Jackson 5, actors George Stanford Brown and Lawrence Hilton Jacobs and featured BKF champion Lenny "Whirlwind" Ferguson. All throughout the 1970s and 1980s, the work of the BKF did not go unnoticed. Among other things, they worked within the black community on behalf of underprivileged children and at martial arts tournament events.

Figure #42 - In addition to being a fierce competitor and tournament champion, Donnie Williams, seen in this match against John Natividad, became a skilled diplomat who opened doors for many BKF students in the professional worlds of music and motion pictures. Below, he stands with long-time friend, writer/director Oscar Williams.

Courtesy of Donnie Williams and Capt. Wildman

In addition to public events and tournaments, BKF co-founder and champion Donnie Williams was a bona fide ambassador who continued to develop alliances for the BKF. As a martial arts instructor and friend to major Hollywood celebrities such as composers Issac Hayes, Jerry Fielding, Artie Kane, screenwriter Sterling Silliphant and writer/director Oscar Williams *(Figure 42)*, Williams helped move the BKF into professional circles within the entertainment community. His skill for diplomacy would add to the legacy of the BKF with the writing of the book *"Championship Kenpo"* in 1983. That book, which was re-issued in 2001, became the nation's first published and internationally distributed martial arts instructional book written by African-Americans *(Figure 43)*.

Figure #43 - The premier publications written by African Americans in the U.S. are *"Championship Kenpo"* (1983), from Ohara Publications, and *"The BKF Magazine"* (2000), from CFW Enterprises. Both were made possible through the vision and pioneering efforts of Donnie Williams.
Courtesy of Nijart International

A few years later, in January 1987, through the diligent efforts of first generation BKF student and archivist Kraiguar Smith, the BKF and several founding members received commendations from Los Angeles Mayor Tom Bradley on behalf of the citizens of Los Angeles *(Figures 44,45)* for years of community service by the Black Karate Federation.

Figure #44-45 - In this 1987 photo, the Honorable Mayor Tom Bradley (center) presents one of many commendations to the Black Karate Federation for their dedication and service to the Los Angeles community. Standing, left to right, are Ron Kim, Steve Sanders, Cliff Stewart, Donnie Williams, Mayor Tom Bradley, Ted Taylor and an unidentified participant. Seated from the left are Jerry Smith, Kraiguar Smith and Angelo Jackson.

Courtesy of Kraiguar Smith

City of Los Angeles

COMMENDATION

WHEREAS, **THE**

Black Karate FEDERATION

AN ORGANIZATION DEDICATED TO PROMOTING FAIRNESS ON THE MARTIAL ARTS TOURNAMENT CIRCUIT, WAS FOUNDED IN 1969 BY STEVE SANDERS, JERRY SMITH, DONNIE WILLIAMS, CLIFF STEWART, AND RON CHAPEL; AND

WHEREAS, THE BLACK KARATE FEDERATION ACTIVITIES ARE CREDITED WITH PAVING THE WAY FOR MORE EQUITABLE REPRESENTATION OF ALL RACES IN TODAY'S MARTIAL ARTS; AND

WHEREAS, THE PURPOSE OF THE ORGANIZATION, STILL STRONG TODAY, IS TO SOLIDIFY THE BLACK POSITION IN TOURNAMENT KARATE THROUGH A STRONGER VOICE IN MATTERS OF JUDGING AND COMPETITION POLICY. THE BLACK KARATE FEDERATION ALSO WORKS TO PROMOTE MARTIAL ARTS AS A VEHICLE TO KEEP BLACK YOUTHS OFF THE STREETS; AND

WHEREAS, THE BLACK KARATE FEDERATION HALL OF FAME AWARD IS TO RECOGNIZE THE GREAT ACHIEVEMENTS BY THE FOUNDERS, TEACHERS AND MANY CHAMPIONS OF THIS PIONEERING ORGANIZATION. ALSO FOR THOSE WHO LIVE UP TO THE STANDARDS CREATED BY THE BLACK KARATE FEDERATION TO MAKE THE MARTIAL ARTS, WHICH ARE BASED UPON UNDERSTANDING, HARD WORK AND A TOTAL COMPREHENSION OF SKILLS KNOWN AS A BETTERMENT OF PRODUCTIVITY IN ONE'S EVERYDAY LIFE.

NOW, THEREFORE, I, TOM BRADLEY, MAYOR OF THE CITY OF LOS ANGELES, ON BEHALF OF ITS CITIZENS, DO HEREBY COMMEND THE BLACK KARATE FEDERATION AND ITS FOUNDERS FOR ITS MANY CONTRIBUTIONS IN PROMOTING FAIRNESS IN THE FIELD OF MARTIAL ARTS; AND

FURTHER, EXTEND BEST WISHES FOR YOUR CONTINUED SUCCESS IN ALL FUTURE ENDEAVORS.

JANUARY, 1987

Tom Bradley
MAYOR

In the field of martial art excellence, when we recall of the notable achievements of the BKF in point or full-contact competition, it was martial artists such as Vountria Moss, Frank Nitty, Al Harvey, Samuel Pace, Al Canister, Ernest "Mad Man" Russell, Ricky Heath, Gary "Crusader Rabbit" Goodman, Gerald "Choo-Choo" Mays, brother Charles Mays, Nathan Cruise, Reginald and Mark Bowden, Eddie "Iron Man" Horton, Freddie Humble, Alvin and Melvin Hilliard, Cynthia Prouder, Terry Dent, Alvin Prouder and many, many others who have had their techniques honed to perfection by Steve Sanders, Jerry Smith, Cliff Stewart, Ron Chapel and Donnie Williams. It is they who have all laid the groundwork and contributed to the BKF Kenpo principles used by BKF champions and taught by BKF instructors internationally *(Figures 46, 46a)*.

Figure # 46 - BKF male and female teams were developed in the early 1980s to compete on a regular basis. Left to right are Lenny Ferguson, Ernest Russell, Gary Goodman, Samuel Pace and James Honest. *Courtesy of Samuel Pace*

Figure # 46a - "The Million Dollar Ladies" are (from left) Lana Prouder, Phyllis McNeal, Cynthia Prouder, Stephanie Prouder and Sharon Floyd. *Courtesy of Samuel Pace*

JERRY SMITH

As times change, new challenges and new needs arise. The core group of the BKF founders have moved on to create new forms of martial expression. Jerry Smith became one of the first full-contact fighters and coaches in American sport karate. Mr. Smith was also an original staff member for *Black Belt* magazine in the 1960s when the magazine was no larger than the popular African-American publication *Jet Magazine*. Mr. Smith was hired by the company's founder and publisher, Mito Uyehara, as a graphic design artist. Jerry Smith currently resides in Sunnyvale, California and teaches for a local high school. He is also the creator and instructor of the 5 Level Method martial art system *(Figure 47)*.

RON CHAPEL

Figure # 47 - Jerry Smith (right) and BKF full-contact fighter Kraiguar Smith. Jerry became one of the best full-contact trainers in the sport.
Courtesy of Kraiguar Smith

Dr. Ron Chapel returned to the American kenpo path established by Ed Parker. As one of the most knowledgeable proponents of American kenpo today, Dr. Chapel teaches Advanced American Kenpo Concepts at the Martial Science University he has founded. Dr. Chapel shares his vast knowledge of locks, submission holds and bio-electrical nerve stimulation. Dr. Chapel places emphasis on the complete understanding of the scientific, mechanical, and physiological principles that regulate human movement and underlie each kenpo technique *(Figure 48)*.

Figure #48 - Dr. Ron Chapel, with his Advanced American Kenpo Concepts, is one of the most knowledgeable instructors on American kenpo today.

Courtesy of Ron Chapel

CLIFF STEWART

Cliff Stewart is the founder of a method of combat known as "Within Arms Reach" or "W.A.R." Having received certification in a number of different systems such as Wally Jay's small circle jiu jitsu, *pentjat silat* and judo, Stewart is also a qualified firearms instructor, professional bodyguard *(Figure 49)*, author and certified instructor in several disciplines, including pentjat silat.

Figure #49 - Cliff Stewart (center) continues to study and teach several disciplines, as he refines his highly effective martial art way known as "Within Arms Reach" (W.A.R.)   *Courtesy of Nijart International*

KARL ARMELIN AND CURTIS PULLIAM

Karl Armelin, a former lieutenant in the U.S. Army, has continued his community service and has been with the Los Angeles Police Department for the past 25 years *(Figure 50)*. He is assigned to a special unit dealing with Los Angeles gangs. Curtis Pulliam *(Figure 51)* has retired from training.

Figure #50-51 - Karl Armelin and Curtis Pulliam are members of the "Magnificent 7" and co-founders of the Black Karate Federation. Today, Armelin (left) is less active in the martial arts but remains a member of the Los Angeles Police Department. Pulliam (right) has since retired from training.   *Courtesy of Carvis Atrice Baldwin and Karl Armelin*

THE BKF PATCH

The patch and logo that identifies the Black Karate Federation today is an amalgamation of several influences of its time. For example, a small, oval-shaped patch, approximately three inches long with a black fist in the center, exists from Willie Short's Kobayashi Karate school. The "B" on that BKF patch reportedly meant "Brotherhood." Falling safely somewhere between the older term Negro and the more radical term black, brotherhood was dropped in favor of "Black," which was adopted by a younger generation as a term of pride and empowerment. A subsequent design by Jerry Smith in 1969 included a fist, as well as additional symbols derived from the struggle and pride within the African-American community *(See page 52).*

Throughout the years, the patch has undergone various modifications before settling in its final form. On the original patch, a sleek cobra arose from the apex of four concentric coils. The red, black and green banner was drawn horizontally across the shape of a fist, which was drawn in outline. In another manifestation, an Asian-style font, on the left of the cobra, was added that said "Kenpo." On the right was the word "Karate." An enlarged painting of this logo, created by visual artist and BKF Kenpo champion Samuel Pace, provides the backdrop for the *"Enter The Dragon"* karate school scene *(Figure 22).*

In the early 1980s, the words "Kenpo Karate" were removed and replaced with the words "Wo Ying Chuan." In Chinese, this means, "Law of the Invisible Fist." Following this, a reference to kenpo returned on the patch in honor of master Ed Parker. Several other versions have been in existence over the years, although unofficially. Today, as the organization now represents more of an amalgamation of styles and systems with kenpo at its center, all wording except for the letters BKF have been removed. This represents the official BKF Kenpo patch and logo *(Figure 52).* In its final form, the logo and patch are more close to the original concept envisioned for the organization in 1969.

TM

Figure #52 - The official logo of the
Black Karate Federation.

*The BKF name and logo are trademarks of Steve
Muhammad and Donnie Williams. All rights reserved.*

THE FIST

In various martial arts systems, the clenched fist is frequently
depicted, just as you would see in reference to goju-ryu karate. The
fist is used by the BKF for the simple reason that the word kenpo
means "Fist" Law. However, the fist as a symbol of power and righteousness is not unique to the martial arts.

During the 1968 Olympic Games, it acquired great cultural significance for blacks when sprinters Tommie Smith, who won the

gold medal in the 200-meter dash, and his teammate John Carlos stood on a podium to receive their awards. In a move that created global awareness for their cause, the runners, with their right hand clad in black gloves, raised their clenched right fists above their heads to protest racism in America. That image has permeated our national consciousness and since that time, for African-Americans and other so-called minorities in America, the image of the fist symbolizes power to fight injustice, as well as the determination to overcome racism.

Through an evolving symbology in BKF kenpo, the knuckles on the fist also symbolize the concepts of yin and yang or complimentary opposites with its concave and convex outlines. The hollow, concave area between the knuckles are the softer, rounded-in areas. The knuckles, which are the convex areas of the fist, are hard. They arch and bulge out. United, they present the fist as a formidable weapon. This symbolism also refers to the original internal and external properties of the science of kenpo. The color gold in the fist symbolizes wealth and power.

RED, BLACK AND GREEN BANNER

The red, black and green banner surrounding the fist represents the Pan-African flag. The legendary Pan-Africanist and freedom fighter, the honorable Marcus Mosiah Garvey, designed this red, black and green flag. Along with the members of the Universal Negro Improvement Association (UNIA) and African Communities League (ACL) of the World, the flag was a part of their Declaration of Rights at their first international convention on August 13, 1920. The UNIA-ACL knew that Africans at home and abroad needed their own symbol as other flags around the world could not represent the collective African people. This symbol was a bold and powerful vision by a black man in an attempt to unify his people. Garvey's inspired work was an example of strategy and also how his strategy was countered.

Most people are unaware that during Garvey's rise, a young and ambitious J. Edgar Hoover, director for the Federal Bureau of Investigation (FBI), hired James Wormley Jones, code-named "Confidential Agent 800," as the FBI's first black agent. What was Wormley's assignment? He was to infiltrate the UNIA and gain Garvey's trust so he could obtain information for the FBI. The FBI later used this information to eventually destroy Marcus Garvey and his movement.

As Garvey envisioned it, the significance of the colors are as follows: red represents "the blood which men must shed for their redemption and liberty." Black represents "the color of the noble and distinguished African people" and green is for "the luxuriant vegetation of Motherland Africa." The colors have since been adopted by an assemblage of 25 countries of the African diaspora, thereby making the colors international. The red, black and green flag represents all peoples of Africa, regardless of land of birth.

THE COBRA

The cobra, which is one of the world's most deadly snakes, strikes with blinding speed. These snakes are found in most of Africa and India, and it has been said that Steve Muhammad's movements are easily reminiscent of the swift and deadly cobra.

Although the use of the cobra on the BKF patch was not consciously made to connect the Black Karate Federation to ancient Kemet or India, it is significant to note that as kenpo originated with blacks, the symbol of the cobra was also used by blacks throughout history.

Known as the "Uraeus" in Kemet, the cobra was used extensively by the Pharaohs. It was also used as a symbol for the pineal gland in the brain, which many refer to as the "third eye" *(Figure 53)*. The cobra was used by the ancient Dravidians in India to represent the process of achieving enlightenment with the rising of the life force with proper training through several energy centers or

Figure #53 - The royal Pharaohs of Egypt, the yoga masters of India and Black Karate Federation practitioners in America have all used the cobra as a symbol of physical, mental and spiritual excellence. This symbol, on three continents, links BKF Kenpo to the oldest martial arts traditions on Earth. *Courtesy of Nijart International*

chakras in the body. This life force rises from the base of the spine to the crown chakra at the top of the head. In ancient Kemet, the life force is known as "Ka" as in Ka-ra-te. It is otherwise known as "kundalini" or "serpent power" in India. The Buddha is often depicted seated in a lotus position on a coiled cobra. In China, this life force is known as "chi." In Japan, it is called "ki."

THE SCROLL

The red scroll beneath the fist represents knowledge. In ancient Kemet, countless volumes of books were written on scrolls of papyrus (from which we get the word paper). The correct knowledge, along with the study and application of that knowledge, allowed our ancestors to create a glorious civilization. This practice of study was again taken up with the African Moors in Spain during the Middle Ages. They created the first universities in Europe. For the practitioner of BKF Kenpo, the scroll is a reminder to study and apply knowledge to understand the who, what, where, when, and why behind the art and science of BKF Kenpo.

BKF CREEDS

There are three creeds or statements of belief used within the BKF. Ed Parker wrote the first. It is as follows:

"I come to you with only karate, empty hands. I have no weapons, but should I be forced to defend myself, my principles, or my honor, should it be a matter of life or death, of right or wrong; then here are my weapons, karate, my empty hands."

Bruce Lee wrote the second creed. It is as follows:

"Be composed, but don't stand still.
Be mobile, but don't move.
Don't attack, strike.
Hit your opponent on his first move.
Move only to counter or attack.
Don't stand still, and yet don't move."

Donnie Williams wrote the third creed:

"Karate is my skill.
I will defend my friends and loved ones to the end.
When I present myself day or night,
They will always know I will walk, run, then fight."

THE BKF CADENCE

Reflecting the military experience of the founders, group cadence chants are used by BKF instructors to lead a school while they run or jog as a team. Cadence also helps to develop rhythm, as well as group cohesiveness and fighting spirit. Following is one such cadence:

Instructor: I don't know, but I've been told...
(school):   I don't know, but I've been told.

Instructor: BKF fights mighty bold.
(school):   BKF fights mighty bold.

Instructor: Am I right or am I wrong?
(school):   Am I right or am I wrong?

Instructor: The BKF fights too, too strong.
(school):   The BKF fights too, too strong.

NEED FOR SURVIVAL

The need for survival is a driving force for all living beings. From the earliest humans who used sticks and stones, to modern man and his strategic use of nuclear and bio-genetic warfare, there may never be an end to conflict or a quest for survival. Throughout the ages, from Africa to America, expressions of human activity that create such entities as the Black Karate Federation are products of centuries of struggle and evolution that will no doubt continue to provide a foundation for future generations to build upon.

The strategy used by grandmasters Steve Muhammad and Donnie Williams since the early days of the BKF in Los Angeles has been to focus on cultivating mental and physical discipline and to be able to use that discipline and apply it to all walks of life, particularly in the area of spiritual growth. They have realized that without a healthy spirit, one's body, one's house, one's community and one's nation cannot endure *(Figure 54)*.

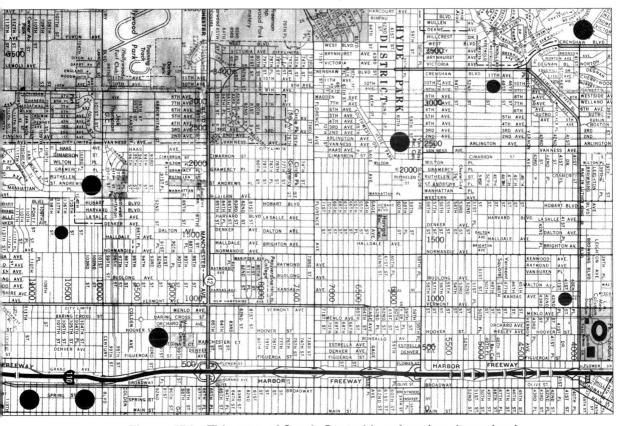

Figure #54 - This map of South Central Los Angeles shows landmark locations of the BKF history throughout several generations.

Courtesy of Nijart International

References: Binns, Nijel. (1990). "*Nuba Wrestling™: The Original Art*"
Higgins, Godfrey. (1833). "*Anacalypsis,*" Vol.1-2.
Newberry, Percy E. (1893). "*Beni Hasan,*" Vol 1-4.
Oyama, Mas. (1958). "*What Is Karate?*"
Parker, Ed. (1960). "*KENPO KARATE, Law of the Fist and the Empty Hand*"
Parker, Leilani. (1997). "*Memories of Ed Parker*"
Rajshekar, V.T. (1987). "*Dalit. The Black Untouchables of India*"
Rashidi, Runoko. (1985). "*African Presence in Early Asia*"
Sanders, and Williams. (1983). "*Championship Kenpo*"
Web sites: **www.theBKF.com, www.BKF-International.com** and **www.Nijart.com**

CHAPTER 2

MASTERS
OF STRATEGY

Between two opponents of equal strength and skill,

it is often the one with superior strategy

who will emerge victorious.

Therefore, Advanced Strategic Principle No. 2 is ...

Know your opponent.

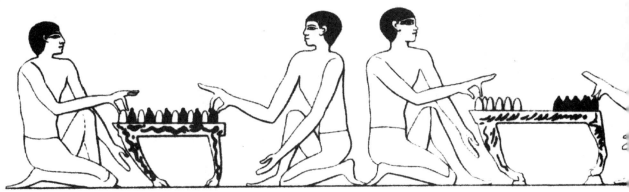

Courtesy of Nijart International

Ask any of the dozens of illustrious champions and warriors throughout the Black Karate Federation's history what was one of the initial strategies they were taught, and he or she will tell you, "Study the opposition."

As we have already pointed out in Chapter 1, when the BKF began, practitioners from several styles and systems met and freely exchanged ideas and techniques. Whenever a BKF fighter would face an opponent in the ring, more than likely, he was already familiar with the fighting style of that opponent. In addition to being familiar with a multitude of martial arts styles, BKF warriors would always bring a little something extra ... street fighting skills with an attitude.

While this may have earned some BKF fighters the title of "street brawlers," they knew as Bruce Lee would become famous for advocating, that in the reality of combat, you use whatever works. Consequently, where many traditional kenpo stylists understood the theories of kenpo, the BKF kenpo stylists were actually able to apply their skills and make them work in the real world. Because of the knowledge and experience that were developed on the streets of Los Angeles, BKF fighters were known and respected by local gang members and law enforcement alike for being able to fight equally well on the street and in the ring.

Throughout history, there have been many leaders and military geniuses who have reaped great dividends by successfully studying their opposition in regulated, as well as unregulated, combat situations. This strategy is a skill that must be developed.

SENET

As an exercise in cultivating strategic thinking, various games have been associated throughout history with strategy and warfare. From ancient Kemet, we see many illustrations of people playing a board game known as "senet." It is a game similar to back-gammon and chess. In one such painting, two men sit facing each other with a small table between them. There are rows of game pieces in front of them. One set of game pieces are white, and the other is black. Both players have their hands on a game piece and are preparing to move. In the adjoining illustration, the game is apparently underway as we see the game pieces intermingled on the board *(See page 88)*.

STRATEGY

Figure #55 - The Moors of medieval Spain played chess as a pastime. Playing chess is known to develop strategic and analytical thinking skills.
Courtesy of Nijart International

Games of this type are found throughout history. In China, evidence seems to suggest that a game known as Hsiang Chi or "image chess" developed there around 561 AD. This was during the reign of Emperor Wu of the Northern Chou Dynasty. That game was a sort of divination activity in which small objects were thrown on a board that had images which represented celestial bodies such as the sun, moon, stars, etc.

During the Middle Ages in Spain, chess among the noblemen was a favorite pastime. There can be no doubt that the 800-year rule of Spain by the Moors, which began in A.D. 711, was made possible through effective strategic thinking skills, the type of which can be cultivated through the practice of challenging games such as chess *(Figure 55)*. Martial artists today can benefit from playing games such as chess, which can enhance their appreciation of, and ability to, apply strategic thinking in daily life.

Several individuals throughout history have exemplified the principles of strategic thinking and the study of the enemy in combat. One such individual was Pharaoh Ramses II. His battle at Kadesh stands as one of the first fully recorded military strategic events in history.

RAMESES II AND THE BATTLE OF KADESH

Kadesh was an ancient city on the Orontes River, located in modern day Tall An-nabi Mind of Western Syria. It was the site of the most well-known battle in ancient times, "The Battle of Kadesh." This location is mentioned for the first time in Egyptian sources when Thutmose III (1479-1426 B.C.) defeated a Syrian insurrection under the leadership of the prince of Kadesh at Megiddo in Palestine. Kadesh remained an outpost of Egyptian influence until it came under Hittite rule around 1340 B.C. Then, in 1275 B.C., Kadesh became the scene of a famous battle between Rameses II and the Hittite Prince Muwatallis *(Figure 56)*.

Seeking to recapture the Hittite-held city of Kadesh in Syria, Rameses II invaded Syria with four divisions and an auxiliary force. Rameses' plan was to send a particular section of his army called the Na'arn, northward along the Phonecian coast, while the main army, which was divided into four divisions (Amun, Pre, Ptah and Seth), marched through Canaan and approached Kadesh from the south. The army of Rameses consisted mostly of soldiers from Kemet, with a few Nubian contingents, and some Sheriden (also known as Sardinian) mercenaries and recruits from Amurru. The chariots were manned exclusively by Kemetic noblemen.

Prince Muwatallis gathered a large alliance among his vassal states, numbering 2,500 chariots and 37,000 infantrymen, which was more than double the size of the army that Rameses commanded. Muwatallis hid his army behind the city mound and sent out false reports that he was at Aleppo, a location farther north. Rameses fell into the trap and rushed his army toward Kadesh with

Figure #56 - Rameses the Great is one of the most celebrated builders and military figures in all of ancient Kemet. The Battle of Kadesh in 1274 B.C. is one of the first and largest commemorated battles in the history of art.

Courtesy of Nijart International

his units stretched along the Orontes Valley road.

Toward evening, Rameses reached Kadesh with his first division and set up camp. It was during this time that two captured Hittite scouts confessed the actual trap that Muwatallis had laid. The Hittites forded the river and, after routing the second division, stormed the Kemetic camp. With his first division destroyed, Rameses was saved mostly by his auxiliary force that struck the attacking Hittites in the rear. Pushing the Hittites into the river, the mauled soldiers retained the battlefield. The next day, a pitched battle was fought, which Rameses claimed for a great victory.

Even though the failure of Rameses' campaign was a result of a tactical mistake by not sending enough scouts to explore the countryside sufficiently, he knew his opponents would not be able to match his faster, more maneuverable war chariots. In addition to this, the courage of Rameses himself enabled his outnumbered Kemetic army to stave off defeat and at least reach a stalemate with the Hittite army.

Along with being a lesson in great military strategy, the battle at Kadesh is one of the largest battle subjects in the history of art. It has been recorded on a great tableau in the temple of Abu-Simbel in both sculpted relief, as well as poetry. The poem that recounts Rameses II's victory at Kadesh is the most celebrated masterpiece of Kemetic literature.

HANNIBAL BARCA AND THE BATTLE OF CANAE

The great Hannibal Barca *(Figure 57)*, was born in 247 B.C. in Carthage, in what today is Tunisa, Africa.

Hannibal's Phoenician name, Chenu Bechola, means "Grace of Baal." His family name, Barca, comes from the Phoenician word that means "thunder bolt." Hannibal had accompanied his father, Hamilcar Barca, on his military campaigns in Spain at the tender age of nine. The Carthaginian general agreed to take his son on the condition that Hannibal swear an oath of eternal enmity against their enemy Rome.

When Hannibal took command of the Carthaginian army at age 25, his goal was the complete destruction of Rome before it could destroy Carthage. The Romans never imagined for an instant that Hannibal could, or would, make a journey of 1,500 miles to accomplish his goal. But that is exactly what he did. He traveled from Spain, across the Pyrenees, through the south of France, and over the Alps into, Italy. Having decided on his strategy and selected his theater of operations, Hannibal followed two principles that have grown no less important since his day: seizing the initiative and

Figure #57 - Hannibal Barca of Carthage was born in 247 B.C. His victory at Canae is the most studied military strategy in all of warfare — past and present. Hannibal handed Rome one of its most crushing defeats. More men died in this battle than in any other single encounter in recorded history.

Courtesy of Nijart International

maintaining the element of surprise.

Hannibal collected detailed logistical information about the people and countries through which he intended to pass. He sent for messengers (liaison officers) from the Gaul tribes and asked for detailed accounts of the terrain and the fertility of the country at the foot of the Alps, in the midst of the Alps and in the plain of the river Po.

Hannibal practiced political intelligence gathering by researching the number of the inhabitants in the various areas, their capacity for waging war, and most importantly, if they were enemies of Rome. He was particularly anxious to win over the Gauls on both sides of the Alps, as he would only be able to operate in Italy against the Romans if the Gauls joined him. He carried out a planned campaign of psychological warfare to raise and maintain the morale of his supporters and to undermine the enemy's will and power to resist.

In one of Hannibal's most famous encounters, the Battle of Canae in Italy, Hannibal faced an opposing Roman army twice the size of his own. Romans relied on their superior numbers and their fighting skill. Hannibal's plan at Canae called for his cavalry of about 35,000 seasoned troops, including a squadron of 21 elephants, to be positioned on the flanks of a crescent-shaped line. Hannibal moved to defeat the Roman horsemen quickly and to attack the Roman infantry from the rear as it pressed upon a weakened center of Spaniards and Gauls. His superior African troops, at the crucial moment, pressed from the flanks and completed the encirclement. Using what has become known as the "double pincer" maneuver, nearly 80,000 Roman soldiers perished within the space of a few hours on a field the size of New York's Central Park. More men died in this battle than in any other single encounter in recorded history. Napoleon is quoted as having rated Hannibal first among the seven greatest generals of all time.

The African influenced Roman republic that followed, along with the advance of the Huns, foreshadowed the eventual Moorish invasions of A.D. 711.

THE MOORS

The Moors were black Africans who adopted the religion of Islam. They lived in North Africa in the country of Morocco, which was named after them. In fact, the word "Moor" means black. Derivatives of the word moor appear in many surnames throughout Europe such as Murray, Moore, Schwartz and Schwartzenegger.

Beginning in the year A.D. 711, General Tarik Ibn Ziad led 10,000 Moorish troops from Africa into Andalusia, Spain. At the location of his landing, there is a towering rock that was named after him to commemorate his victory. It is known as "gebel el Tarik" or more commonly, "The Rock of Gibraltar."

STRATEGY

During the period of Moorish rule in Spain that spans 800 years, Spain became the center of learning and excelled in everything from the arts and sciences, to medicine and literature. The Moors introduced 17 universities in Europe at a time when Europe had none. They had hot and cold running water. Their architecture provided scented air conditioning for the homes by allowing cool air to pass over a banks of flowers as it entered the home. The success of the Moors can be attributed in large measure to the knowledge and technology borrowed from their predecessors, the Nubian and the Kemites whose influence stretch far back in time. In fact, the Black Pharaoh of the 25th Kemetic Dynasty (Taharka) led Kemetic troops into Spain five centuries before the Moorish invasion of A.D. 711.

The military strategy of the Moors included the building of fortifications, use and development of armaments, hand-held blades and spears, as well as firearms. The Moors pioneered the use of hand-held cannons, which became the forerunner of the modern bazooka. Not only did the Moors usher in a new level of military excellence, but they also had a highly enriching cultural influence on all of Europe and set the stage for the Renaissance or "re-birth" that was to come.

When the Moors conquered Spain, they brought many wonderful gifts and riches to the Spanish people and to all of Europe. They introduced rice, coffee, oranges, sugar and spices. They also taught the Spanish a new way of farming called "strip farming." They introduced irrigation and water management and developed a way to store wheat for 100 years. They introduced new scientific inventions like the water wheel, hot and cold running water, mathematics, Arabic numbers, as well as the concept of the university, the public library and public baths. Scholars have often said that had the Empire of the Moors survived, human kind would be at least 500 years more advanced than people today *(Figure 58)*.

Copyright 2002
Nijil

Figure #58 - The 800-year rule of the Moors in Spain began in A.D. 711. The Moors relied not only on military strategy, but also by advancing learning for all people in art, literature, science, medicine and agriculture.

Courtesy of Nijart International

STRATEGY

SHAKA ZULU

King Shaka kaSenzangakhona of the amaZulu in South Africa is one of the most famous African leaders of the 19th century. Born in 1787, Shaka grew to be a young man of daunting physical strength and a commanding personality.

Shaka came to the throne in 1816 at a time when his clan was largely unknown. By the time of his assassination 12 years later, his power extended over hundreds of square miles. Now, in all fairness to King Shaka and the amaZulu, it must be noted that the Zulus were not a war-loving people. Vusamazulu Credo Mutwa, the renowned Zulu High Sanusi or High Priest said, "Zulu people actually hated war and didn't love it as historians would have you believe. We Zulu people call war "impi," and we called evil "imbi" or "woobi." Now the word imbi and the word impi come from exactly the same root, which means "that which is evil." We call copper "itusi," which means "the helper, the frightener away of evil spirits." But we call iron "incimbi," which means "the evil metal, the metal of war."

As a military leader, King Shaka saw the need to institute many changes in the manner of warfare waged by his predecessors. Before Shaka's arrival, Zulu battles in the 19th century followed a ritual that consisted of an exchange of throwing spears at the enemy, followed by a retreat to await the enemy who would throw spears back. Shaka did away with this and instituted close-combat fighting. He made his warriors throw away their many spears, or "assegais" and ordered each man to carry only one.

Shaka devised a new weapon that was a short, broad-bladed stabbing spear that he called "iKlwa." It was a stabbing and thrusting weapon instead of a throwing weapon. The shield or "isihlangu" that each warrior carried was enlarged to offer protection to the entire body. When Shaka engaged an enemy, he would use his shield to batter the enemy. Then, he would hook it over the edge of his opponent and drag it to the left. The enemy would be thrown off balance (his own shield blocking his movements) and his left side open and exposed to Shaka's thrusting spear. With this one movement, he was protecting himself from the last spear in his opponent's right hand and, at the same time, exposing the man's left armpit to the thrust of his stabbing spear *(Figure 59)*.

Shaka developed an attack formation called the "impondo

Figure #59 - King Shaka Zulu was born in 1787 and was one of the most famous African leaders of the 19th century. His revolutionary weapon designs, training and fighting strategies enabled him to consolidate many separate Zulu clans to mount a strong defense against the invading British. *Courtesy of Nijart International*

zankomo" or "beast horns" strategy. A strong army of senior warriors, known as the "chest," advanced in close order until they were almost upon the enemy. Then, young warriors known as the "horns," who were on either flank, ran around the enemy and surrounded them. The central group of experienced warriors then advanced and crushed the enemy against the anvil of the "horns." Behind the chest was the "loins," a reserve of experienced warriors. Shaka was an inspired tactician and a stern and aggressive commander. He was never afraid to strike hard and strike fast. This was the attitude that he cultivated in each of his warriors.

STRATEGY

Shaka's discipline of his army was an important part of his overall strategy. Before Shaka took command, the army was unaccustomed to running. They wore oxe-hide sandals and lacked the stamina to go great distances. Also, their mobility was hampered by the sandals. Shaka did away with sandals as he himself had done. From then on, his warriors all ran barefooted with him and marched each day for 20 miles over rugged terrain. This built great stamina and endurance.

When Shaka's army engaged their enemy, they ran in formation swiftly to the attack with their shields tucked under their arms. They would bring them out when they got within range and then run in a stooping position, increase their speed and converge upon the enemy with unmatched fury. Shaka's strategy focused on discipline, superior weapons technology and fighting techniques.

STEVE MUHAMMAD AND DONNIE WILLIAMS

During their days of tournament competition, the fighting strategy employed by BKF warriors Steve Muhammad and Donnie Williams enabled them to achieve victory after victory in hundreds of matches throughout their career. It was an effective blend of speed and power that proved to be the winning combinations in their matches.

From the start of his career as a martial arts competitor and instructor, Muhammad became well-known for the lightning fast execution of his techniques, both in training and in combat. As a former track runner, Muhammad realized that his fast-twitch muscles allowed him to execute techniques and movements much faster than those of his opponent. While training, Muhammad laced every technique with speed and power. He realized early on that a realistic and effective training method should be one in which each and every movement should be executed with maximum speed and power. He fought as he trained.

Steve Muhammad's development of training and fighting principles, such as "brain sight," combined with his superior speed, enabled him to detect his opponent's movements well before they were actualized. In combat, this valuable asset allowed him to be an effective counter fighter, one who relies on the opponent to present the openings and pathways for an attack.

For Donnie Williams, the most effective defense proved to be an exceptionally strong offense. There were numerous battles and tournament victories in which Donnie Williams entered with a stronger will and determination than that of his opponent. On one hand, as a physically commanding figure, Donnie Williams mastered the strategy of silent as well as vocal intimidation. Whereas an opponent might expect to be out maneuvered and fall victim to the speed and power of Steve Muhammad, Donnie Williams' opponents knew — in a glance — that he was out to hurt them.

Besides this, Donnie Williams also used humor to disarm an opponent. He would occasionally joke with an adversary. Once the opponent no longer felt threatened and relaxed even slightly, Williams would unleash the full force and power of his techniques and simply overpower the opposition.

Figure #60 - As fearsome warriors and martial art tournament champions of the 20th century, Steve Muhammad and Donnie Williams honed their strength, discipline, superior technical skill and a sense of mission to uplift black people through the kenpo martial sciences.
Courtesy of Geri Simon

As warriors, Steve Muhammad and Donnie Williams studied the opposition and knew their opponent well *(Figure 60)*. As students and teachers, they studied themselves and knew their strengths and weaknesses. Both fighters understood the need to tailor their techniques to fit both their body types, as well as their personalities, and made use of this to enable them to become successful throughout their careers. They continue to research, refine and impart this knowledge to the hundreds of students they have taught.

CHAPTER 3

WARM-UP AND GENERAL CONDITIONING EXERCISES

You can know your opponent's strengths and weaknesses and

still lose a fight because you do not know your own.

Therefore, Advanced Strategic Principle No. 3 is ...

Know yourself.

Constant, repetitive training in the 12 basic moves and techniques such as those outlined in *"Championship Kenpo"* made it possible for BKF warriors such as Steve Muhammad and Donnie Williams to remain sharp, focused and able to call upon their skills at a moments notice. All great fighters throughout the ages have spoken of the need for mental, physical and spiritual conditioning through steady, repetitive training.

Mental conditioning, as we have seen in the earlier chapters, can be developed through the study of history, as well as understanding how to apply those lessons of history to the art and science of kenpo. Physical conditioning involves the practice of a variety of techniques such as stretching, calisthenics, and breathing exercises that are designed to strengthen the body and prepare it for martial arts training. Physical training should not be taken for granted.

In Chapter 1, if you recall, we spoke about Bodhiharma introducing breathing and conditioning exercises to the sedentary monks at Shaolin. The need for specific exercises to maintain and strengthen the body in the 6th century is no less important for the martial artist today in the 21st century. Remember, the human being is a combination of mental, physical and spiritual energies. To leave any one out of a person's overall development is to be out of balance. This imbalance can result in a lack of ease in one's life and can lead to disease, which manifests itself in the form of cancers, heart disease and a host of other ailments. These could be avoided through simply devoting time to developing the physical self.

Some martial arts practitioners abuse their physical selves by trying to enhance their bodies with synthetic drugs and other means. Other martial artists neglect their physical selves and become grossly out of shape and unhealthy internally.

The martial arts are a wonderful science. To truly master them takes a lifetime of discipline. Furthermore, if we believe that the body is a temple and house for the spirit, then the proper care and maintenance of the body cannot be overlooked.

There are a variety of exercises that are illustrated on the following pages. You should read through them carefully. In a few of them, such as the sit-ups and push-ups, you will notice that they have an added dimension in the use of cadence or rhythm. The

CONDITIONING

practice of performing exercises to rhythm dates back to ancient Kemet. Many illustrations throughout Kemet depict men and women going through various exercises while musicians keep a beat by clapping to a rhythm or playing a musical instrument *(Figure A)*. Ancient African cultures understood that there is rhythm in everything in the universe. Nothing is at rest, even if it appears to be absolutely still. Even on the subatomic level, there is motion. Everything is in motion. To become a successful martial artist, and more importantly, a successful human being, you must learn to cultivate an understanding of "rhythm in motion."

Through the practice of simple sit-ups and push-ups performed with a beat, BKF training has achieved a good measure of success by introducing basic rhythms that provide the foundation for students to go on to develop more sophisticated and complex rhythm patterns in their fighting techniques. Some BKF kenpo practitioners have become interpretive in the physical execution of their techniques and their complex rhythm patterns ... much like a jazz musician.

Figure #A - In this illustration, the ancient people of Kemet perform various exercises while musicians keep a beat by clapping and playing a musical instrument.

Courtesy of Nijart International

In its purest form, kenpo is dynamic and fluid; it is never stagnant. Steve Muhammad is primarily responsible for bringing BKF kenpo to this level of a sophisticated motion-based, rhythm-laced science and art. To observe his fluidity of movement, timing and blinding bursts of speed, it is clear that there are complex rhythm patterns at work on top of — and intertwined with— his kenpo techniques. In addition to this, all of these elements, according to him, are operating subconsciously. To get more insight into this, as well as rhythms and additional ways to develop rhythm, refer to Chapter 6.

JUMPING JACKS

In the BKF, jumping jacks are done in unison with the class while counting off numbers to the instructor's lead. Training in this way builds rhythm as well as team comraderie. Read through the steps below and study the illustrations carefully to get a full understanding of the rhythm patterns you are about to practice.

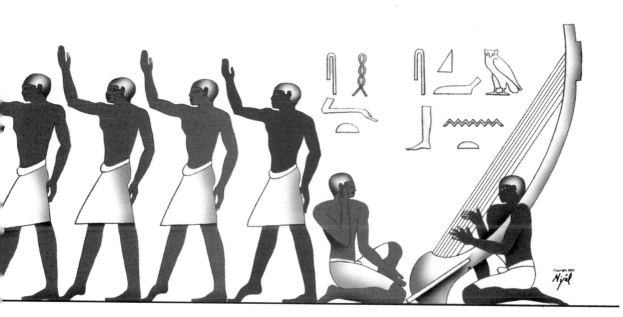

CONDITIONING

JUMPING JACKS

1. Stand with your feet together and your hands at your sides.
2. On the first jump, count "One!"
3. On the return, count "Two!"
4. On the second jump, count "Three!"
5. On the return, count "One!"

This constitutes one repetition or "rep." Repeat steps two through five. On the return, count "Two!" This now constitutes two reps. Continue steps two through five until you reach 30 reps.

SHOULDER SHRUGS

1. Stand with your feet shoulder-width apart and your hands at your sides.
2. Rotate your shoulders up.
3. Continue rotating your shoulders up and back.
    4. Return to the starting position.

Repeat by rotating the shoulders five times going up and back and then five times going up and forward.

CONDITIONING

SIT-UPS (Part A)

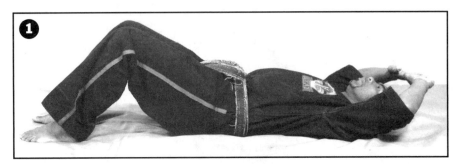

In the BKF, sit-ups are also performed to a set rhythm pattern. In a basic sit-up routine of 30 reps, the first 10 will follow a specific pattern *(Part A)*, while the remaining 20 will follow a different pattern *(Part B)*.

For the first 10 reps *(Part A)*:

1. Lie on your back, feet together, knees drawn up and hold your hands overhead.

2. Sit up and clap both hands on the count of "One!"

3. Slap the mat with both hands on the count of "Two!"

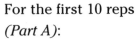

4. Clap both hands together on the count of "Three!"
5. Lie back down to the count of "One!"

This constitutes one rep. Repeat steps two through five. On the return, count "Two!" This now constitutes two reps. Continue steps two through five until you reach a total of 10 reps. You will go to a more advanced rhythm pattern from reps 11 through 30.

CONDITIONING

SIT-UPS (Part B)

For reps 11 to 30 *(Part B)*, do the following:

1. Lie on your back, feet together, knees drawn up and hold your hands overhead.

2. Sit up and quickly clap both hands together twice.

3. Slap the mat with your left hand.

4. Slap the mat with your right hand.
5. Clap both hands together once.
6. Lie back and count

This sequence constitutes one repetition. Repeat the above sequence (steps one through five) until you reach a count of 30 reps.

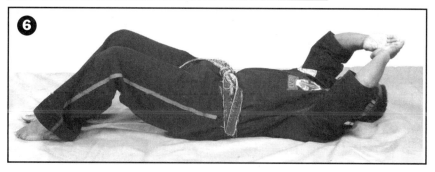

SIT-UP VARIATION (Part C) Elbow to Knees

1. Lie on your back, fold your hands behind your head and hold your knees up. This time cross your right foot across your left thigh.

2. Sit up and bring your left elbow toward your right knee.

3. Lie back down.

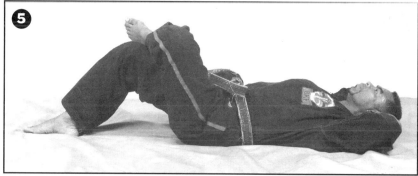

4. Sit up and bring your right elbow toward your left knee.

5. Lie back down. Continue this sequence from left to right until you reach your maximum number of repetitions.

CONDITIONING

SIT-UP VARIATION (Part D) Crunch

1. Lie on your back, fold your hands behind your head and hold your knees up.

2. Lift your head and shoulders off the mat and exhale as you crunch your abdominal muscles.

3. Breathe in, as you lie back down. Repeat this sequence until you reach your limit.

PUSH-UPS

Push-ups are done to strengthen the arms, chest and upper body. There are several varieties of push-ups that can be performed, such as regular, wide palm, one-on-one, inverted push-ups, etc. They should be performed vigorously and with good breathing.

REGULAR PUSH-UPS

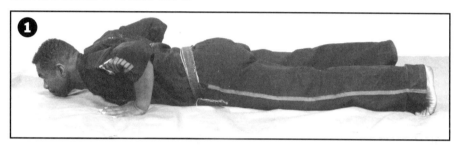

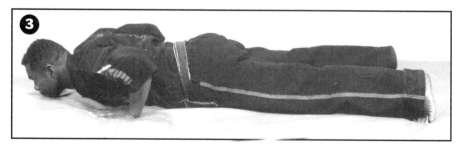

1. Lie on your stomach with your hands on the floor at chest level.

2. Breathing out, push up off the floor.

3. Breathing in, lower your body back to the floor. Repeat for three sets of 20 repetitions.

CONDITIONING

WIDE PALM PUSH-UPS

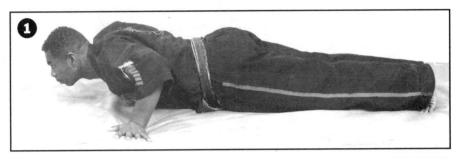

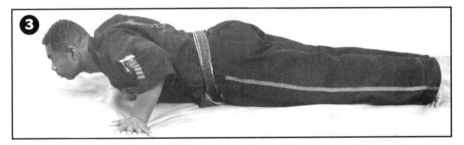

1. Lie on your stomach with your hands on the floor about 14 inches from your body. Point your fingers away from your body.

2. As you exhale, push up off the floor.

3. Inhale as you lower your body back to the floor. Repeat for three sets of 20 repetitions.

INVERTED PUSH-UPS

1. Assume a push-up position with your hands at stomach level. Point your hands and fingers toward your toes.

2. Breathing in, lower yourself to the floor.

3. Breathing out, push yourself back up into a push-up position. Repeat for three sets of 20 repetitions. This variation is an excellent exercise for the forearms.

WRIST PUSH-UPS

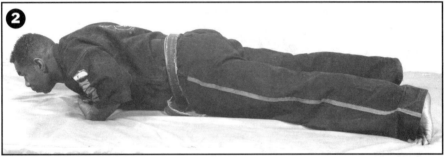

1. Assume a push-up position on your wrists.
2. Breathe in as you lower yourself to the floor.
3. Breathe out and push yourself back up into a push-up position. Repeat for three sets of 20 repetitions. This variation strengthens the wrists.

CHAIR PUSH-UP #1

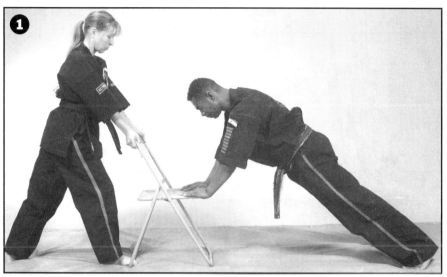

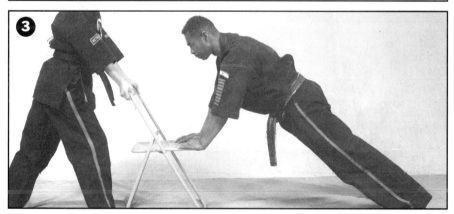

1. For this version, you'll need a chair and a partner. Place your hands on the seat of the chair, extend your legs out behind you and have your partner hold the chair.

2. Lower yourself toward the seat.

3. Push up and away from the seat. Repeat these movements for three sets of 20 repetitions. Do not forget to breathe.

CHAIR PUSH-UP #2

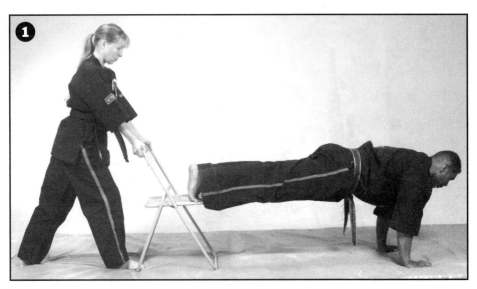

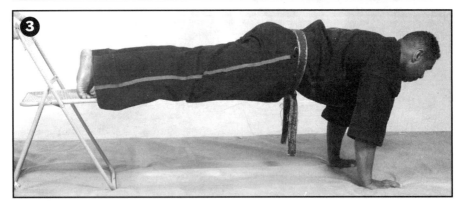

1. This time you'll put your feet on the seat and your hands on the floor. Again, your partner should hold the chair.

2. Lower your body to the floor.

3. Push up back to your original position. Repeat with gusto for three sets of 20 repetitions.

TRICEPS EXTENSIONS

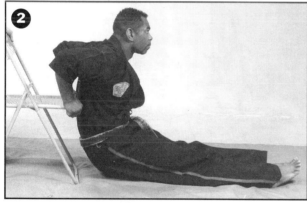

1. You will again need a partner and a chair for this exercise. To begin, sit on the edge of the seat, place your hands on the seat and extend your legs in front of you. Your partner should again secure the chair.

2. Bend your elbows and lower yourself to the floor.

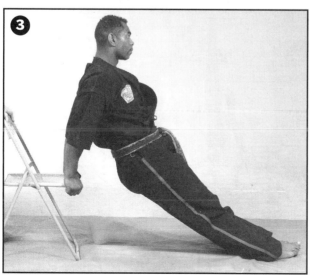

3. Push back up and recover to the starting position. For added benefits, contract and tighten the triceps at the top of each motion. Repeat for three sets of 20 repetitions.

CONDITIONING

WRIST/FOREARM ROTATION EXERCISE

1. Stand with your feet at least shoulder-width apart or more. Grasp a pole in the center with your outstretched hands, parallel to the floor.
2. Begin to rotate your left hand over your right.
3. Continue until the pole is again parallel to the floor.
4. Reverse the rotation back to the starting position. Repeat this exercise on both sides, in opposite directions three times.

SPINE AND BACK EXERCISES

The spinal column (backbone) is the most important series of bones in the human and animal body, because it has bundles of nerves that originate from the brain, down the spine and out throughout the entire body. The spinal disks are stacked on top of one another, or in a row, with the nerves coming out between them. As we age, the spaces between the disks begin to compress due to a lifetime spent under the influence of gravity. When this happens, the nerves between the disks get squeezed and this slows the flow of impulses from the brain to the limbs and other parts of the body. If you want to keep your body youthful and flexible, and keep your mind sharp, you will pay attention to your spine. There are several exercises, such as the plough and the cobra from the Indian practices of yoga, that help to keep your spine flexible. Another good exercise is the spinal twist.

CONDITIONING

SPINAL TWIST

1. Sit on the floor with your legs stretched out in front of you.

2. Place your left leg over your right.

3. Place your left hand behind you and bring your right hand over your left knee and down to the knee of your extended foot.

4. Using your right arm to brace yourself, breathe out as you twist to the left as far as you can comfortably go. Hold that position for a five count. Relax, breathe in and return to the starting position. Wait five seconds and repeat. Eventually, you should be able to hold this position comfortably for several seconds before releasing. Repeat these movements on the opposite side. Again, pay attention to your breathing.

CONDITIONING

COBRA

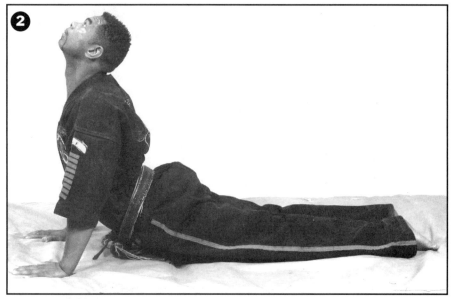

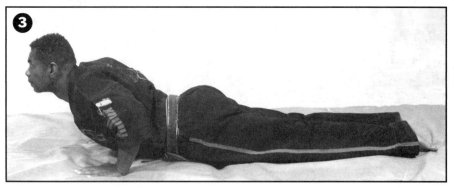

1. Lying face down on the mat or floor, place both hands to your side at chest level.

2. Breathe in as you lift your upper body off the mat. Keep your back arched and head up. You should feel the stretch in your lower back. Hold for a count of five before releasing your stretch.

3. Breathe out as you slowly lower yourself back to the mat. Repeat this sequence three times.

PLOUGH

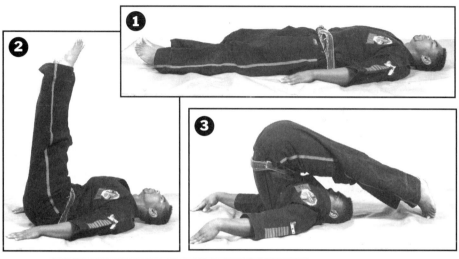

1. Lie on your back with your palms down at your sides.

2. Inhale and lift both feet until your legs form a 90-degree angle.

3. Exhale as you bring both feet down to the mat.

4. For an added stretch, lower your knees to the mat.

5. Recover by breathing in as you lift your feet off the mat.

6. Exhale as you lower your straight and outstretched legs to the mat. Repeat this exercise twice.

CONDITIONING

SIDE BENDS

1. Stand with your feet shoulder-width apart and your hands to the sides.

2. Bend at the waist to the right.

3. When you reach the limit, gently stretch in that positions for two or three seconds.

4. Return to the starting position and repeat on the left side. Repeat this exercise on both sides three times.

TRUNK TWISTING

1. Stand with your feet shoulder-width apart or more and wrap your arms around a pole that you balance across your back.

2. Twist your upper body to the left.

3. Continue until you reach your limit. Gently stretch in that position for two to three seconds.

4. Return to the starting position and repeat on the left side. Repeat this exercise on both sides three times.

CONDITIONING

TRUNK TWISTING VARIATION

1. Do this gently to avoid straining your lower back. Stand with your feet shoulder-width apart or more and hold a pole across your back.

2. Bend forward at the waist until your torso is parallel to the floor.

3. Begin to twist your right shoulder to the floor.

4. Continue until the pole and your shoulders are vertical.

5. Recover to the starting position and repeat on the left side. Repeat this exercise on both sides three times.

LEG STRETCHING EXERCISES

To achieve a good stretch, you must breathe properly, monitor your body for proper relaxation and go slowly. These are the important points to keep in mind as you approach the following exercises.

ALTERNATE SQUATS

1. Stand with your feet about two times the width of your shoulders and place your hands on your knees.

2. Keeping your right leg straight, squat to the left. If done properly, you will feel a mild stretching of your right inner thigh muscles.

3. Repeat this movement on the other side.

4. Return to your starting position and repeat the above sequence five additional times.

ALTERNATE HAMSTRING STRETCHES

1. Stand with your feet about two times the width of your shoulders and place your hands on your knees.

2. Squat on your left leg, keeping your right leg straight as you did in the previous exercise. However, in this exercise point the toes of the extended leg straight up.

3. Return to the starting position.

4. Repeat the squat on the other side.

ALTERNATE LUNGES

1. Again, stand with your feet two times the width of your shoulders.

2. Place your hands on your hips. Rotate your trunk to the right. When you do this, you should bend your right knee and twist your left leg, which should be kept straight. You should also be on the ball of your left foot.

3. Return to the first position.

4. Repeat this to the other side.

Repeat this sequence five additional times. Each time try to stretch just a little farther.

STANDING ALTERNATE HAMSTRING STRETCHES

1. Stand with your feet two times the width of your shoulders.

2. Bend forward at the waist. Keeping both legs straight, try to touch your head to your right knee.

3. While still lowered, switch and try to touch your head to your left knee. Repeat this sequence five times on both sides. Each time try to stretch just a little more.

BUTTERFLYS

1. Sit on the floor and hold your feet together.
2. Exhale, grasp both feet, keep your back straight, and lower your chest and head toward your feet.
3. Inhale and return to the starting position. Repeat this sequence five times. Be sure to breathe properly. The key to this exercise is keeping your lower back straight.

SINGLE-LEG SEATED HAMSTRING STRETCH #1

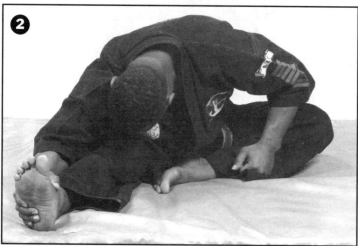

1. While seated, extend your right leg and pull the sole of your left leg toward your groin.

2. Grasp your right ankle or — if possible — your right foot, and exhale as you lower your head to your knee. Make sure you keep your back straight. Inhale and return to the starting position. Repeat several times with the right leg extended before you switch to the left side. Again, the key here is to maintain a straight back.

SEATED HAMSTRING STRETCH VARIATION

1. While seated, extend your right leg and pull your left foot and knee back behind your body.
2. Grasp your right ankle or — if possible — your right foot. Exhale as you lower your head to

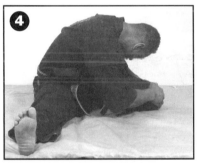

your knee.

3. Inhale and recover to the starting position.
4. Grab your left knee. Exhale as you lower your head to your knee.
5. Inhale and recover to the starting position.
6. For an extra added stretch, carefully and slowly try to lie back on the mat with your left leg folded. Repeat several times with the right leg extended before you switch to the left side.

OPEN-LEG SEATED HAMSTRING STRETCH

1. Sit on the ground with both feet spread as far as possible.

2. Grasp your ankles, exhale and lower your head to the floor. Hold for five seconds.

3. Taking shallow breaths, move your torso over your right leg. Touch your head to your knee and hold for five seconds.

4. Move your torso over your left leg, lower your head to your knee and hold for five seconds.

5. Inhale and return to the starting position. Repeat this sequence three times.

CLOSED-LEG SEATED HAMSTRING STRETCH

1. Sit with both legs together in front of you.
2. Keeping your back straight, grasp your ankles, breathe out, lower your head to your knees and hold for five seconds.
3. Inhale and return to the starting position. Repeat this sequence four times.

CONDITIONING

THIGH AND TORSO STRETCH

1. Kneel on the ground, keep your back straight, your knees open and point your toes. Slowly sit back on your lower legs.

2. Using both arms to brace yourself, carefully lower your head backward onto the mat.

3. Keeping your back arched, try to relax and allow your torso, thighs and pelvis to stretch.

4. Use your arms and upper body for support and return to the starting position. Repeat twice.

JUMP ROPE VARIATIONS

Everyone is familiar with jumping rope. Boxers use this exercise to develop stamina, hand and foot coordination, rhythm and timing. The basic jump rope exercise is performed in three two-minute rounds of jumping. On the last 30 seconds of each round, the jumper picks up the pace to maximum speed and "burns" out the remaining time. The following jump rope exercises will provide variations to the basic jump rope theme and will help to improve your footwork beyond the basic rope jumping routine. These variations can also be performed for one-minute time intervals before returning to the basic jump rope pattern for the remaining minute.

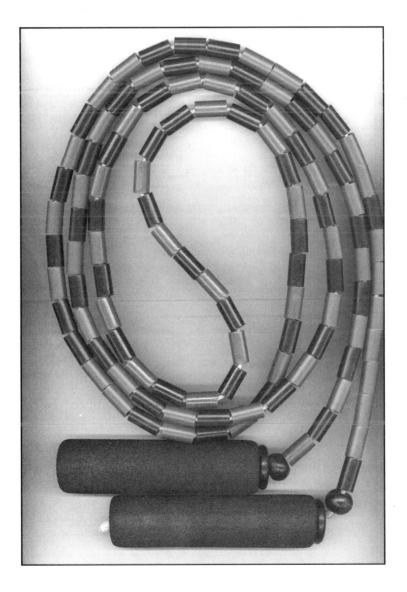

CONDITIONING

JUMPING JACKS

1. After establishing a regular rope jumping rhythm, add jumping jacks to the routine and continue for 30 to 60 seconds before moving to another jumping jack variation.

JUMP ROPE LUNGES

1. While jumping rope normally, add lunges by alternately shifting your right and left foot forward using a regular, consistent, walking rhythm.

CONDITIONING

JUMPING ROPE SKI VARIATION

1. While jumping rope, keep both feet together and alternate a hop from left to right and back. Continue this teeter-toter, left-and-right motion for 30 to 60 seconds before moving to another jumping jack variation.

JUMPING ROPE CROSS STEPS

1. While jumping rope, spread your feet apart and then cross your right foot in front of your left and jump back out. On another count, cross your left in front of your right and jump back out. Continue this quick cross-stepping variation for 30 to 60 seconds before stopping.

CONDITIONING

JUMPING ROPE TORSO TWIST

1. While jumping rope, twist your legs and hips to the right, keeping your upper body centered.

2. & 3. Then, twist your lower body to the left.

4. Twist back to the right. Continue to alternate side to side for 30 seconds before ending the routine.

THE KEY TO TRAINING

There is no single exercise, routine or gimmick that is complete for the maintenance and development of the human body. Because the human body is a complex organism of millions of parts, the key to training is variety. In addition to the exercises just presented, there are also breathing exercises that will develop internal energy and strengthen the internal organs. You must research these exercises and use them to compliment the active, external muscle building exercises you have just practiced. After all strenuous exercise sessions, it is advisable to practice breathing and relaxation before going on to study the techniques in the following chapters.

CHAPTER 4

COMBAT SPECIFIC DRILLS

In the art of war, when all is said and done,

you either win, lose, survive or perish.

Therefore, Advanced Strategic Principle No. 4 is ...

If it works, use it.

As we have pointed out in the last chapter, constant and repetitive training in the basics make it possible for BKF warriors to remain sharp and focused. At the same time, however, as a warrior, it is one's duty to "study" the art and science of fighting. Often, a martial artist will learn a few techniques and will not go beyond these techniques to understand other forms of combat. In the BKF, this approach was never taken.

Steve Muhammad, in the early days of the BKF, not only served as a catalyst to bring martial artists of different styles together so that they could all learn from each other, he often visited many schools and worked out with the classes, whenever possible. He knew that when it came to tournament competition or street application he would stand a greater chance of being successful if he were familiar with and capable of utilizing a specific technique or movement that he had seen.

Today, throughout the martial arts community, there is a greater awareness of the need for a comprehensive approach to training that will enable a practitioner to understand the totality of combat. Grappling, knowledge of nerve stimulation and *kata* (forms) are completing the martial art knowledge base of BKF kenpo, thereby enabling the martial artist to become more well-rounded in his discipline.

In the following examples, techniques are given as drills to be performed that will enhance your knowledge and application of nerve strikes, joint locks, holds and throws.

THE BKF SALUTE

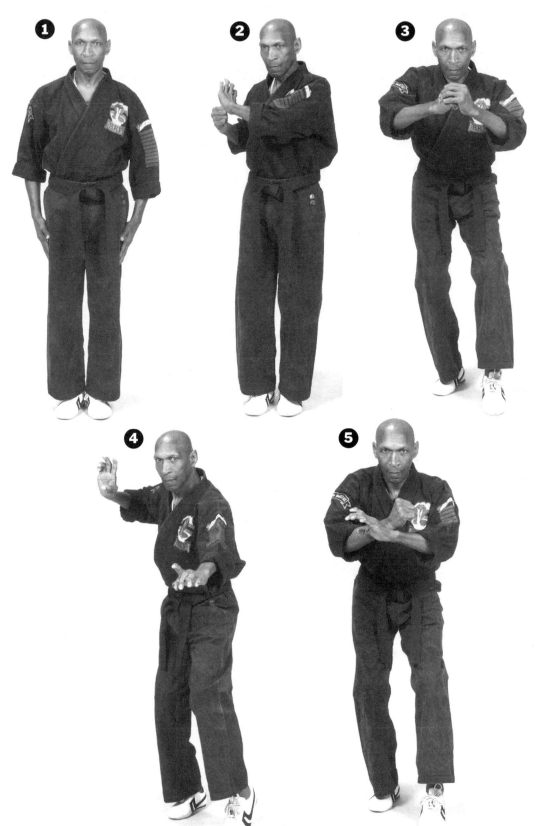

1. Stand in a neutral position, feet together and hands to the side.

2. Pull the right fist, covered by the left palm to the right side of the body. The right hand symbolizes the weapon while the left hand symbolizes the shield.

3. Step forward into a cat, or light leg stance with the left foot, then bring your hands forward.

4. Pull the right fist, or hand back while extending the left hand forward.

5. Bring the hands together, right fist behind the left forearm. This is interpreted to mean, "I won't fight you, but if you force me, I will."

6. & 7. Step back into a neutral stance with your left foot while extending your arms overhead and out to the side in a circular arch.

8. The arms come down to the sides, and the hands slap the thighs to end the salute.

TECHNIQUE #1

1. Face your opponent from a right on-guard position.

2. As the opponent steps forward with a right punch to your face, parry with a right, opened-hand block.

3. Pivot right and execute an outside left-hand check.

4. Grip your opponent's wrist with your left hand, pivot left and simultaneously hit him with a right rising forearm strike under his right biceps.

5. Step forward with your right foot into a low horse stance and strike with a right forearm smash to the midsection.

6, 7. Step back into position, pull your opponent's hand down and strike him with a right elbow under the chin.

8. Prepare to execute a throw. Begin by circling your arm clockwise around your opponent's neck.

9. Push the opponent's right arm back as you continue to circle your right arm around the neck.

10. Execute the throw by thrusting your right arm forward, as you release the opponent.

COMBAT DRILLS

TECHNIQUE #2

1. You are caught in a choke from behind. Secure your opponent's arm and pull it away from your neck to create room to manouvor.
2. Raise your left foot.
3. Stomp down hard on your opponent's foot (In training, use power, but control so you don't hurt your partner).
4. Recoil your leg.
5. Kick your opponent's instep and simultaneously

begin to secure opponent's wrist.
6. Grab your opponent's wrist in both hands and extend your opponent's arm overhead.
7. Pull your opponent's arm down forcefully over your shoulder for an armbar (elbow break).
8. Maintain a grip on your opponent's wrist with your right hand, pivot into your

opponent and hit him in the midsection with a left elbow.
9. Secure his wrist with both hands as you cross-step to the rear with your left foot.
10. Pivot left as you apply a wrist lock to your opponent's extended arm.
11. Step forward for a left front kick to the face.
12. Recoil the leg, and finish with a left side kick to the back of the knee.

TECHNIQUE #3

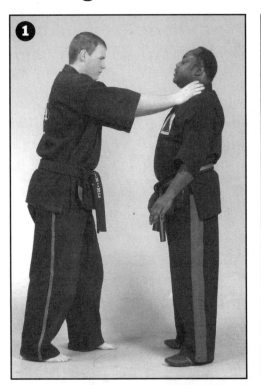

1. You are caught in a choke from the front.

2. Grip the opponent's right hand with your left hand and simultaneously strike with a right-hand spear thrust to the throat.

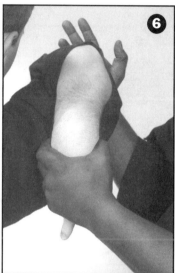

3. Follow with a downward finger strike to the throat and begin to execute a wrist lock so you can release the choke.

4. Step forward with your right foot for a wrist and elbow lock.

5. Continue the twisting motion, lifting the opponent's elbow up and his wrist down.

6. Wrist/elbow lock close-up.

7. Finish with a takedown.

COMBAT DRILLS

TECHNIQUE #4

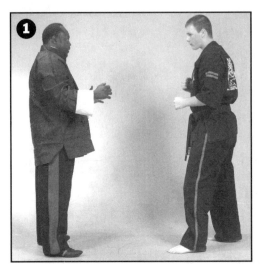

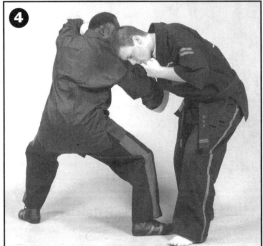

1. You are facing an aggressor who is about to attack.
2. Step away from a right hook while blocking with your left hand.
3. Secure the opponent's hand at the wrist, pivot left and execute a right upward strike under the biceps.
4. Right step into a low horse stance while striking to the opponent's mid-section.
5. Grab the opponent's wrist in your right hand and pivot counter clockwise.
6. Step into your opponent with a left elbow to the ribs.
7. Bring the opponent's arm overhead in front of you as you begin to lift your left knee to strike.
8. While pulling down on the opponent's arm, come up with a left knee to the elbow.
9. Follow with a left side kick to the instep.
10. Continue with a left front kick to the face.

TECHNIQUE #5

1. An aggressor grabs you at the collar with his right hand.
2. Secure his grip with your left hand.
3. While maintaining your grip on opponent's wrist, pivot right.
4. Reverse pivot and hit him with a right hammer fist to the upper pectorals.

5. Right step into a low horse and strike with a right hammer fist to the side.

6. Step up and away from him and grab his wrist in both hands overhead.

7. Maintain a left hand grip on the opponent's arm and raise your left foot.

8. Execute a left side thrust kick to the ribs.

TECHNIQUE #6

1. This is from a headlock position.
2. Bring both fists up above your head.
3. Simultaneously throw a hammer fist strike to the thigh and kidney.
4. Shift your left hand through to the front and strike the opponent's face.
5, 6. Use an armbar and push the opponent backward over your left knee.
7, 8. Raise your right fist high overhead and come down with an hammer fist to the opponent's thigh.
9, 10. Finish with a left elbow smash to the throat.

TECHNIQUE #7

1. Using both hands, the opponent grabs your throat.
2. Grip his right wrist with your left hand and throw a right finger thrust to his throat.
3. Attack the trachea with a downward right finger thrust.
4. Twist your opponent's right wrist to the outside with your left hand and strike him inside his right thigh with a right knee.
5. Loop your right arm over opponent's arm for an armbar and wrist lock.
6. Maintain a grip with your right hand on your opponent's right wrist while you step away to your right.

7, 8. Pivot left toward the opponent and hit him in the mid-section with a left elbow.

9. Follow with a left forearm across the throat.

10. Release the opponent's hand and step away to the right. Finish with a left side kick to the chest.

TECHNIQUE #8

1. Face your opponent from a right on-guard stance.
2. Parry the opponent's left jab.
3. Parry a left roundhouse kick.
4. Parry opponent's right roundhouse kick.
5. Parry your opponent's straight right punch with an outward right hand circular block.
6. Step to the left and strike with a left hammer fist to the kidney.

7. Drop low for a right knifehand strike to the opponent's inside right knee.

8. Stand up with your opponent's right arm over your shoulder.

9. Hold opponent's hair with your left hand and his face with your right hand.

10. Sharply twist the opponent's head to the left (do this slowly in practice).

11. Take the opponent down backward and finish with a right strike to the head.

TECHNIQUE #9

1. In a left on-guard stance, face an opponent armed with a knife.
2. Lean back to evade a slash.
3. Quickly move to the left, outside of your opponent's guard, and use your right forearm to block the returning strike.
4, 5. With your right hand, grab the opponent's hand at the wrist. Pivot right, and while securing his wrist, execute a left armbar.

6. While maintaining a grip with the right hand, bring your left forearm over and down on your opponent's biceps, forcing him into a takedown with an armbar.

7. Pull opponent's head back.

8. Finish with a knifehand strike to the throat.

TECHNIQUE #10

1. While facing an opponent armed with a knife, bring your hands up in front of you.

2. As the opponent lunges at you with a right-hand knife thrust, shift to the right and parry with a left hand outward block. Then grab the weapon hand at the wrist.

3. With a grip on the opponent's weapon hand, counter strike with a right open-hand strike to the face.

4. Follow with a pivot to the right and fire a left punch to the face.

5. Continue with a pivot left and a right finger thrust to the throat.
6, 7, 8. Finish with a right punch to the solar plexus and right elbow
to the jaw.

TECHNIQUE #11

1. In a left forward on-guard stance, face an opponent armed with a club (in his right hand).

2. Parry the opponent's strike with your left hand as you shift and pivot to the left.

3. Strike the back of opponent's weapon hand with a right back-knuckle strike.

4. Grab the opponent in a face lock and twist his head to the left (use caution and do this move slowly).

5. Twist your opponent's head back to the right (again use caution).

6. Step back with the left foot, securing the opponent in a headlock.

7. Lift the opponent's head up.

8. Torque right and throw your opponent's head and body by shooting your left arm forward.

COMBAT DRILLS

TECHNIQUE #12

1. Face your opponent in a left foot forward on-guard stance.
2. The opponent throws a right to your chin and connects.
3. Roll with the punch and pivot right.
4. The opponent follows with a right front kick.
5. Cross step left and block the kick with a downward right-hand check.
6. The opponent fires another right to the face, which you right hand parry outward.

9. Step forward with the right foot and drive a right forearm to the ribs.

10. Drop low for a right ridgehand strike to the outer thigh.

11. Step up and bring your right arm up and across the opponent's body.

12. Clasp both hands around your opponent's neck.

13. Pull the opponent backward, over your right leg.

14. Take the opponent down.

7. The opponent fires a second right front kick, which you check with a right hammer fist strike to the foot.

8. The opponent follows with another right to the head. Parry with a right upward block.

TECHNIQUE #13

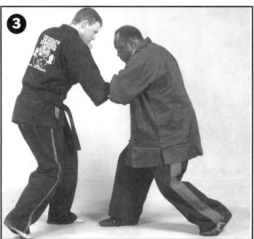

1. Face your opponent in a right-foot forward stance.
2. Parry his left jab outward with a right open-hand block.
3. When your opponent counters with a right to the stomach, parry downward with your left hand.
4. Immediately pivot left and counter with a right hammer fist to your opponent's groin.
5. Throw a headbutt under your opponent's chin.
6. Extend both arms under the opponent's arm.

7. Lift opponent's arms up and out.

8. Simultaneously strike inward to opponent's kidneys with a double hammerfist strike.

9. Grip your opponent around the waist with both hands and throw a headbutt to his sternum.

10. Using the knuckles of both thumbs, apply pressure to the kidney area.

11. Release your grip, step back with your right foot and throw a right punch to your opponent's chin.

12. Finish by pivoting right and hitting with a left punch to the chest.

TECHNIQUE #14

1. Face your opponent from a right on-guard stance.
2. When the opponent steps forward with a right cross, pivot left and counter with a right hand check, left-hand elbow strike.
3. The opponent counters with a left hook, which you parry with a right outward block.
4. Grab your opponent's left wrist with your right hand. Torque right and shoot a left forearm strike to opponent's head and neck.

5. Follow-up with a downward left elbow to the neck.

6. Secure the opponent's left hand and bring your left arm over the opponent's arm.

7. Execute an armbar into a takedown.

COMBAT DRILLS

TECHNIQUE #15

1. Armed with a staff and with your right foot forward, face your opponent, who is armed with a stick.
2. Flip the staff up and to the right to intercept his outward strike.
3. Use the staff to force the opponent's weapon down.
4. Step back with your right foot and strike the weapon hand to force your opponent to drop the weapon.

5. Step forward with your right foot and flip the staff around to strike the opponent's elbow.
6. Flip the staff forward and step left as you follow with a left strike to the back of the head.
7. Pivot left to finish with a right strike to the side of the head.

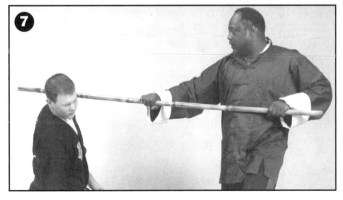

TECHNIQUE #16

1. Assume a right on-guard stance and face your opponent.
2. When your opponent steps forward with a right punch,
parry with a right open-hand check.
3. As the opponent counters with a left punch to your head,
counter with a simultaneous right hand check and left palm
strike to the chest.
4. Follow with a downward smashing, right hammerfist strike
to the collarbone.

5. Continue with a right hammerfist strike to the groin.
6. Come up with a sharp right elbow under the chin.
7. Finish with a pivot left and a right roundhouse kick to the opponent's rear leg.

CHAPTER 5

BKF KENPO SELF-DEFENSE TECHNIQUES

Take the initiative to study kenpo and

improve yourself and your community.

Advanced Strategic Principle No 6 is ...

Define, Develop, and Defend.

BKF kenpo, as an evolving science, has been forged in the reality of street combat since 1968. The effectiveness of BKF kenpo techniques and strategies lie in the fact that they are battle-tested, tried and true. As a self-defense method and martial science, BKF kenpo was refined from, and still is, geared toward application in street combat.

BKF kenpo's "physical" expression applies to street situations first. However, within the context of the street environment, it must be clearly stressed that no attack is 100 percent predictable. Therefore, the reader should not interpret the following situations and responses as the "only" or absolute way to respond to an attack. That would be foolish.

BKF kenpo has been refined to the degree that it is safe to predict with a certain amount of accuracy just how the human body will react "once it is struck." However, you must make allowances for many other variables such as height, weight, possible intoxication, etc. The techniques you will learn will provide you with a framework for developing the confidence to be able to adapt to any situation and emerge from a confrontation victoriously.

Execute the following techniques with focus, precision and power. Training to apply kenpo in a self-defense situation is essentially no different than how it should be practiced in a studio or executed in a tournament. The same intensity and realism should be maintained in all three settings. Of course, you must use control so you don't injure your training partner.

Keep in mind that there should be no part of the human body that you cannot strike with the hand within a fraction of a second. If you practice to make a strike or a kick, you must do so and learn to generate full power so that If — and when — you are called upon to defend yourself, you will be able to do it effectively and with full speed and full power. There are no in-betweens. You cannot use half-power. You can only learn control, which means not touching or barely touching. Control is in the "depth" of the punch or kick when it penetrates the body. Control has nothing to do with the speed or the power of that punch or kick.

Here are some important principles for you to remember before you find yourself in a hostile situation:

1. Never be the aggressor. Try at all cost to avoid conflict. This is the first and most important thought to keep in mind when you face a potentially threatening situation. In today's reality of street violence, you cannot afford to lose your life over foolishness.

2. If an aggressor lays his hands on you, and "only" if an aggressor lays his hands on you, it is your moral and spiritual obligation to defend yourself.

3. You should seek to follow and live by the BKF creeds as outlined in Chapter 1.

SELF-DEFENSE TECHNIQUES
EXAMPLE # 1:

DEFENSE AGAINST A TWO-HAND LAPEL GRAB - Scenario A

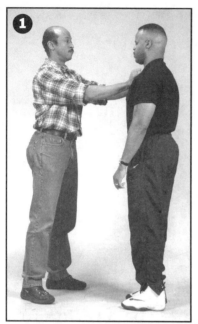

1. An opponent has you in a two-hand lapel grab.
2. Lift both hands up through your opponent's grip, forcing a release.
3. Step forward and strike down sharply with a double knifehand to the collar bone.
4. Pivot left, away from your opponent. Execute a right hammer fist strike to the groin. Your opponent will bend forward in pain.

5. Follow with a right, rising elbow strike under the chin.
6. Execute a quick right scoop kick to the groin.
7. Step away with your right foot, while turning to look over your left shoulder.
8. Throw a left heel thrust kick to the opponent's midsection.

EXAMPLE #2

1. Face the opponent in a neutral, non-threatening stance.

2. When the opponent steps forward to throw a right punch to your face, step off-line to your right and check the blow with both hands.

3. Step forward and strike his ribs with the back of your right hand.

4. Bring your right hand up under your opponent's elbow for an armbar as you simultaneously push down with your left hand.

5. Grab your opponent's wrist with your left hand as you step forward into a right elbow strike to the ribs.

6. Step into the opponent with your right foot. Maintain a grip on his wrist.

7. Throw a right heel kick to his groin.

8. Pivot out on your left leg as you simultaneously shove the opponent backward with your left hand.

EXAMPLE #3

1. Your opponent has you in a headlock.
2. Spread both of your arms out to the side.
3. Simultaneously strike your opponent in the groin with your right hand and the kidney with your left hand.
4. Bring your left hand over opponent's shoulder and around to the face.
5. Stand upright, while pushing your opponent's head up and back with your left hand, forcing him off balance and over your left knee.
6. Extend your right hand to the side in preparation for a strike.

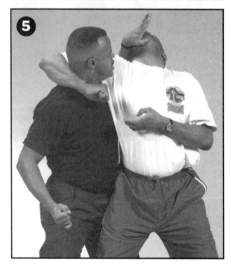

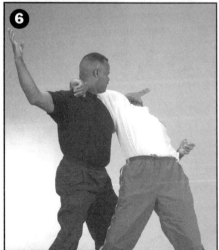

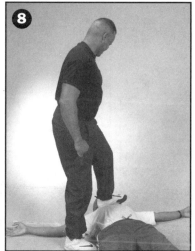

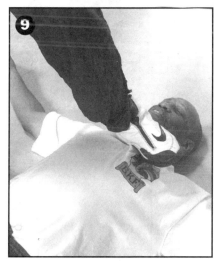

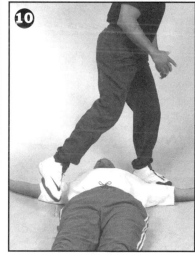

7. Execute a right knifehand strike to the throat.
8. Once your opponent goes down, follow with a left side kick to the throat.
9. A close-up of the throat shot.
10. Step over your opponent with your left leg
11. Execute a quick right kick to the face.

EXAMPLE #4

1. The opponent has you in a bear hug.
2. Secure your opponent's hands with your left hand and shift low to the right.
3. Execute a right kick to your opponent's left knee.
4. Follow with a right kick to the opponent's right knee.
5. Throw a hard, right stomp kick to your opponent's right instep.
6. Step back with your right foot so you are between your opponent's stance.

7. Pivot right and throw a right elbow strike to the side of his head.

8. Reverse pivot and execute a left elbow to the face.

9. Throw a scoop heel kick to his groin.

10. Step away with your right foot and finish with a swift left side kick to the chest.

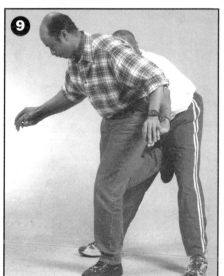

SELF-DEFENSE

EXAMPLE #5

1. Your opponent grabs your throat with his right hand.

2. Reach over his arm with your right hand and grab his hand.

3. (CLOSE UP) As you grip your opponent's hand, your thumb should be on the back of his hand.

4. Using your right hand, pull his hand from your throat. Rotate your opponent's arm down to the right as you push your opponent's elbow with your left hand.

5. Pivot to your right and apply downward pressure with your left hand to your opponent's elbow as you simultaneously step forward with your left foot.

6. Step forward into position with your left foot.

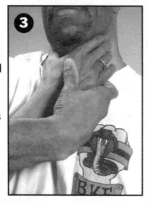

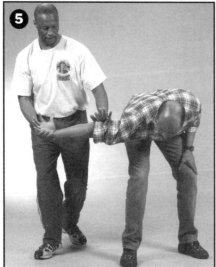

7. Pull your left hand back and prepare to strike.

8. Strike him in the head with your left elbow.

9. While maintaining a grip with your right hand, place your left hand behind the opponent's head.

10. Pull his head down and to the right.

11 Pull him to the ground.

12. Step back from the opponent and into an on-guard stance.

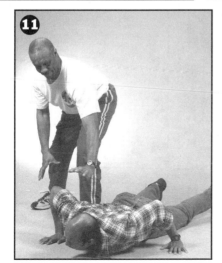

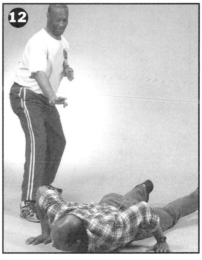

EXAMPLE #6

DEFENSE AGAINST A TWO-MAN ATTACK - Scenario A

1. Your right arm is locked behind you as a second opponent approaches.
2. Intercept the incoming opponent with a quick left leg front kick to the groin.
3. As the opponent leans forward, grab his head with your left hand and throw a right knee to his face.
4. Step back with your left foot.
5, 6. Pivot left so you can throw a left elbow strike to the opponent's head.

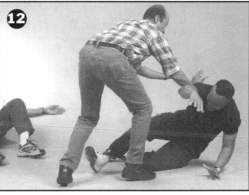

7. Secure opponent's right hand with your right hand as you step away to the right.

8. Continue a 360-degree pivot to your right. Force the opponent to bend forward, and off balance, while you secure his arm at the elbow.

9. Execute a right kick to the mid-section.

10. Move into the opponent while you raise your right hand over your head.

11. Drill him in the spine with a right elbow smash.

12. Push the opponent away.

SELF-DEFENSE

EXAMPLE #7

DEFENSE AGAINST A TWO-MAN ATTACK - Scenario B

1. Two people are on either side. Monitor both of them with your peripheral vision.
2. Check the first opponent's right punch with a right outward block.
3. With the same hand, counter with a right vertical punch to the jaw.
4. Again with your right hand, seize his wrist, pull and fire a short left punch to the ribs.
5. As the opponent shifts backward, cross step forward with your left foot.
6. Execute a quick right roundhouse kick to the groin.

7. Turn to intercept the second opponent's downward strike with a left rising head block.

8. Counter with a right palm strike to the face.

9. Throw a left palm strike to the stomach.

10, 11. Finish with a left side kick to the stomach.

EXAMPLE #8

DEFENSE AGAINST CLUB ATTACK

1. In a left on-guard stance, face your opponent, who is armed with a club in his right hand.
2. Intercept his downward strike with a left rising forearm block.
3. Secure the weapon hand with your left and shoot a right palm strike to the face.

4. Follow with a torquing left palm strike to the ribs.
5. Pivot away from the opponent and finish with a left side kick to the ribs.

EXAMPLE #9

1. While you are in a neutral stance, your opponent attacks with a looping left punch.

2. Step forward with your right foot and simultaneously execute a right rising forearm block.

3. Follow with a right punch to the face.

4. Torque right for a left finger jab to his face.

5. Pivot left for a right hammer fist strike to the groin.
6. Follow with a rising elbow strike under the chin.
7. Finish with a thrusting left palm strike to the chin.
8. Shift back on your left foot for a right kick to the groin.

EXAMPLE #10

1. While you are in a neutral stance, an opponent prepares to step forward with a right cross.
2. Intercept the blow with an open, double-hand check.
3. Counter with a right back hand to the groin.
4. Strike under his chin with the back of your wrist.

5. Reach forward and grab the opponent's neck with your left hand.

6. Pull your opponent's head down and prepare to drill him with your right elbow.

7. Throw a right elbow smash to his upper back.

8. Finish with a right scoop kick to the groin.

EXAMPLE #11

DEFENSE AGAINST A TWO-HAND LAPEL GRAB - Scenario B

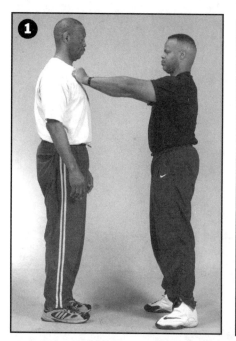

1. An opponent grabs you with a two-hand lapel grab.
2. Step back with your left foot and break his grip by raising both of your hands between his hands.
3. Counter with a left palm strike to the face.
4. With the same hand, throw a palm strike to the chest.

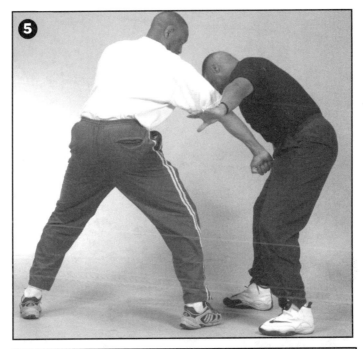

5. Pivot left and hit him in the groin with a right hammer fist.
6. Conclude the sequence with a right front kick to the groin and quickly recover.

EXAMPLE #12

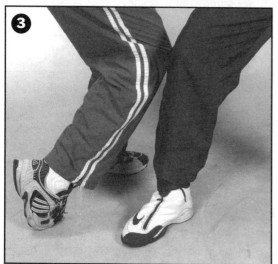

1. In a neutral stance, face your opponent.
2. As he attacks with a right punch, shift left and parry the blow outward with your right hand.
3. With your right knee, block your opponent's lead leg to neutralize his potential to kick.
4. Counter with a right hammer fist to the kidney.

5. Pivot right and execute a left palm strike across the face.

6. Pull his head back with your left hand and pull his right arm back. Prepare to strike.

7. Throw a right knifehand to the throat.

8. Recover on-guard.

EXAMPLE # 13

DEFENSE AGAINST A TWO-HAND LAPEL GRAB - Scenario C

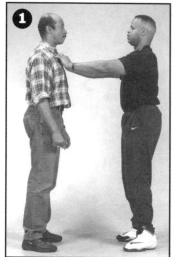  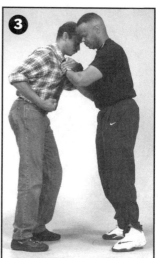

1. You are caught in a two-hand lapel grab.
2. As the opponent pulls you, do not resist.
3. With your left hand, pin your opponent's hands to your chest.
4. Strike with a right punch to the stomach while bringing your left hand across his face.
5. Pivot right and come across the face with a left forearm strike.
6. To break his grip, hit your opponent with a left knifehand strike.
7. Sight your target and pull your right hand back.

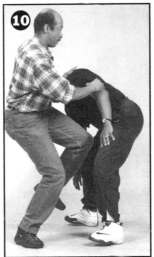

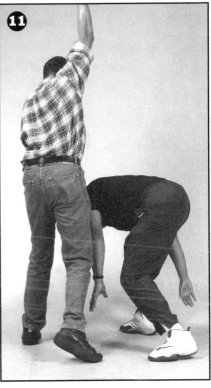

8. Pivot left with a right punch to the face.

9. While positioning his body with your right hand, throw a punch to his stomach with a short left.

10. Kick him in the groin with your left knee.

11. Shift left and raise your right hand over head.

12. Come down with a right elbow strike to the spine. Remember to use control.

13. Push the opponent away and quickly recover on-guard.

EXAMPLE #14

1. Assume a neutral position while facing the opponent.

2. When your opponent throws a right punch, step to the left and parry the technique with your left hand.

3. Counter with a right punch to the ribs.

4. Shift left.

5. Throw a right thrusting side kick to the back of the opponent's knee.

6. Grab the back of his shirt or jacket with both hands.

7. Step back with your right foot. Pull the opponent backward so he is off balance.

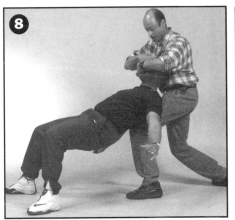

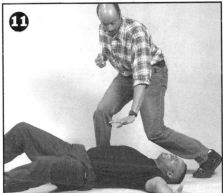

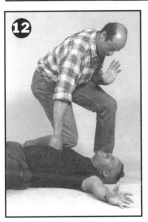

8. Lower your opponent over your left knee. Execute a double-hand face rake.
9. Lift both hands overhead.
10. Strike down with a double knifehand strike to the clavicle or collarbone.
11. Allow the opponent to fall to the ground. Remain on-guard.
12. Finish with a right punch to the solar plexus.
13. Throw a right stomp kick to the throat.
14. Step over the opponent and shoot a left back kick to the face.
15. Recover on-guard.

CHAPTER 6

ADVANCED KENPO FIGHTING PRINCIPLES

The brain, among its many functions,

is the key to movement and rhythm.

Therefore, Advanced Strategic Principle No. 5 is,

Use it, or lose it.

The human brain contains nearly 100 billion brain cells, and these are called neurons. The inner connections in the brain are called "synapses," and they are virtually unlimited. In Webster's dictionary, a synapse (pronounced "sin aps") is defined as the junction point of two neurons, across which an electrical nerve impulse passes. The word "synapse" comes from the Greek. "Syn" means "together," and "haptein" means "to clasp."

The speed at which the human brain can process information is unmatched in our world today. Electrical impulses jump across the synapse and carry information so rapidly, it is amazing. For example, it takes about 100th of a millisecond for the brain to recognize a familiar face on a photograph. Not even the most sophisticated computer is capable of doing this. Then, there is our physical capacity for reading that is beyond our comprehension. Our eyes have the capability to take in a full page of text in 1/20 of a second. These two examples alone just hint at the awesome power and capacity of the human brain. Yet, here is the shocking news... we only use 1/10th of the brain's potential. Why?

Martial artists must continually seek out ways to develop superior brain power. The practice of the martial arts, with its emphasis on being able to perform techniques from either side of the body — as well as other disciplines such as meditation — have been proven to develop the power and potential of the brain. There are a few simple exercises that you can do to stimulate brain function and increase its capacity. They are as follows:

• **One, you can read a sentence backward with understanding.**

• **Two, practice to recognize and read words upside down. There is a supplement on page 218. It is the first part of this text written backward. Use this as an exercise to develop your eye-to-brain power.**

You can also do some hand-to-brain coordination exercises. For example, if you are right-handed, write left handed. If you normally do things with your right hand, do them with your left. It is important to understand that the brain cannot recognize what it does not know. When you are looking forward, you are looking for

THE UNLIMITED POTENTIAL OF THE BRAIN

Technically speaking, the human brain contains nearly 100 "billion" brain cells, called neurons. The inner connections in the brain are called "synapses" and they are virtually unlimited. In Webster's dictionary, a synapse (pronounced 'sin aps,') is defined as the junction point of two neurons, across which an electrical nerve impulse passes. The word "synapse" comes from Greek: "syn" meaning "together" and "haptein" meaning "to clasp".

The speed at which the human brain can process information is unmatched in our world today. Electrical impulses jump across the synapse and carry information so rapidly, it is amazing. For example, it takes about 100th of a millisecond for the brain to recognize a familiar face on a photograph. Not even the most sophisticated computer is capable of doing this. Then, there is our physical capacity for reading which is beyond our comprehension. Our eyes have the capability to take in a full page of text in 1/20 of a second. These two examples alone just hint at the awesome power and capacity of the human brain. Yet, here is the shocking news...we only use 1/10th of the brain's potential. Why?

Martial artists must continually seek out ways to develop superior brain power. The practice of the martial arts, with its emphasis on being able to perform techniques from either side of the body, as well as other disciplines such as meditation have been proven to develop the power and potential of the brain. There are a few simple exercises that you can do to stimulate brain function and increase its capacity. One eye-to-brain exercises is practicing to read a sentence backwards, with understanding. Another is to practice to recognize and read words upside down. At the end of this chapter is a supplement. It is this text written backwards as well as upside down. Use this as an exercise to develop your eye-to-brain power.

Some hand-to-brain coordination exercises are simple things such as practicing to write left handed if you are right handed, or doing things that you normally do with your right, doing them with your left. It is important to understand that the brain cannot recognize what it does not know. When you are looking forward, you are looking for things you only recognize. In fighting, this is why we say that you must know and train the brain for combat. This knowledge comes through study.

The correct application of BKF Kenpo relies on understanding specific principles that will allow the practitioner to apply the science. If you do not have a knowledge of these fighting principles, then combat becomes an inefficient, and ineffective game of tag. Your fighting will be mechanical and lack truthfulness because you will simply be going through the motions. The true science and art of fighting is a thinking man's discipline that countless generations have spent their lives working to perfect.

SUPPLEMENTAL EYE/BRAIN COORDINATION EXERCISE
Recognizing and Reading Words Written Backward

The opening paragraphs to this chapter are written backward. Attempt to read the sentences and recognize the words. This exercise is one way to develop eye to brain coordination.

things you only recognize. In fighting, this is why we say that you must know and train the brain for combat. This knowledge comes through study.

The correct application of BKF kenpo relies on understanding specific principles that will allow the practitioner to apply the science. If you do not have a knowledge of these fighting principles, then combat becomes an inefficient and ineffective game of tag. Your fighting will be mechanical and lack truthfulness because you will simply be going through the motions. The true science and art of fighting is a thinking man's discipline that countless generations have spent their lives working to perfect.

There are many advanced kenpo fighting principles that are utilized in BKF kenpo. Some, for example, fall under a concept known in the BKF as Mathematical Fighting. Others cover body language, Brain Sight, etc. All of these are necessary for the warrior to have an understanding of, so he will be able to utilize them at his command.

BRAIN SIGHT

The concept of Brain Sight is actually a pluralistic concept. It encompasses all of our known senses; therefore, when we speak about it, we can more accurately consider it as Brain "Sights" *(Figure #1)*. There are six principles that define this concept and they should be studied well. They are as follows:

- **The brain has the ability to cause the body to move — with no delay — as it detects an opponent's movement.**
- **The brain also has the ability to create or adapt instantly.**
- **The brain has the ability to respond on impulse, which takes little energy or thought.**
- **The brain cannot be fooled or tricked. Once trained, it can only adapt.**
- **The brain must be disciplined to overcome obstacles — physical or mental.**
- **The brain functions in mathematics — at the level of mathematics— in which you have trained or learned to fight.**

Figure #1 "The brain functions in mathematics — at the level of mathematics in which you have trained — or learned to fight."
— *Steve Muhammad*
Courtesy Nijart International

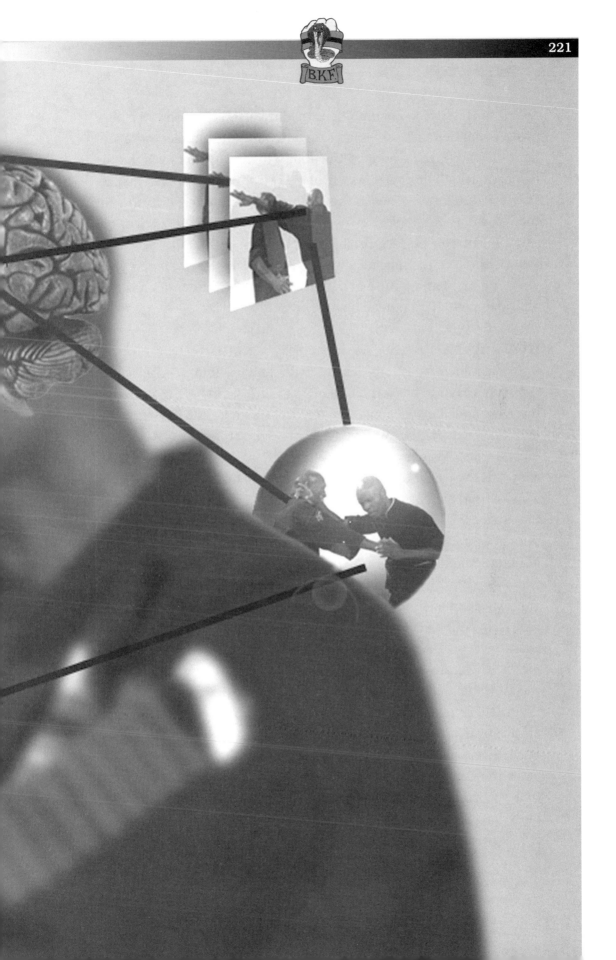

Brain Sight also encompasses the little used extra-sensory perceptive abilities that we all have. In combat, for example, there are fighters who have developed the ability to sense a person's movement and feel their power just by being in front of them, even before they strike. They can sense the opponent's ability to perform and their power to hit. Energy gives off a vibratory wave that cannot be seen, but it can be felt. Brain Sight also takes this into account. More clearly stated, because we are bioelectric beings, if you give your opponent an impulse in action or "thought," the brain has the ability to pick that impulse up.

BODY LANGUAGE

The human body engages in a wide range of activities (walking, running, playing basketball, dancing, etc), and there are specific "vocabularies" for every activity. **The brain sees fast "as" slow.** In the martial arts, body languages vary from style to style and from system to system. It is what allows us to be able to distinguish kenpo from taekwondo, from hapkido and jiu jitsu and so on. Once you have learned the vocabulary and language of an art, there is nothing in combat that an opponent's language of attack can say to you that you will not understand.

It is possible to teach body language through fighting. Once you fight long enough, your body and mind will have the opportunity to master that language. However, you must teach body language slowly. The eyes will have the time to pick up the movements. The brain, on the other hand, does not care how fast or slow the movements come. The brain sees fast "as" slow.

In this stage of learning body language, you must have a cooperative training partner. A partner communicates to you the movements that you will learn to recognize. A training partner also provides the counter movements as answers to the offensive actions that you make. In this way, you will learn to read your partner's body language while he is on the defense. The process of slow fighting teaches the brain. It actually programs the brain through repetition.

Another result of learning and developing the vocabulary of

body language is that this information, once studied, can increase your understanding of the logical sequence of your attacks. You will discover that if you hit the body in a certain way, the body will react at a certain angle. In time, you will be able to read and understand these angles. You will not have to consciously look for these targets because your brain will recognize them when they present themselves in the way that you have trained.

MATHEMATICAL FIGHTING — THEORY AND CONCEPTS

Everything that comes into existence comes into existence through mathematics, even the joining of an egg and sperm and the dividing of the cells that create a human being. Everything follows a mathematical code. In music, there is a mathematical code or rhythm. In fighting, there is also a mathematical rhythm. This is why Muhammad Ali, Bruce Lee and "Sugar" Ray Robinson were such great fighters. They utilized mathematical rhythm. All fighters have a mathematical rhythm, but not all fighters are speaking the body language and mathematical code on the same level. Muhammad Ali, for example, had a mathematical rhythm that allowed him to hit and not be hit.

To illustrate this point regarding mathematical understanding and a musical rhythm in fighting, observe a beginner in the martial arts. Basic or beginning fighters will fight with something close to a rhythm pattern that looks like this: 1 and 2 and 3 and 4. In comparison, advanced fighters move like this: 1234. They seem extremely fast because they leave out the "and" in their mathematical equation.

Master Ed Parker introduced a concept of angles and geometric patterns of movement in kenpo that the BKF expanded upon. The principle behind mathematical fighting is easy to understand. The untrained fighter can express random reflex movements during combat that are not efficient. The purpose of mathematical thinking in combat is to eliminate unnecessary movements. It is that simple. Mathematical fighting focuses on angles and the logic of movements before, during and after an attack.

There are eight fundamental components that will develop an analytical ability that will lead to an increase in your skill, awareness and use of mathematical fighting. They are as follows:

- **Double tapping**
- **Torquing**
- **Walking on the opponent**
- **Hidden moves**
- **Bone-on-bone**
- **Critical distance fighting**
- **Hitting the opponent off the mark**
- **Building momentum on the attack**

Let's now look at teach of these.

DOUBLE TAPPING: This is a technique that supersedes alternating hand rotation punches in critical distance fighting. With double-tap striking, moves can be done with the same hand, two or more times, while generating the same power as you would if your hand rotated, such as in a reverse punch. This technique contrasts with the old days of training at the Crenshaw school, for example, in which BKF students executed combinations and follow-through movements such as the "Over-under, back knuckle, reverse punch." In the following examples, you will see double tap, as well as other principles, such as positioning and torquing.

EXAMPLE #1

1. Assume a right on-guard stance and face your opponent.
2. Parry the opponent's left punch with a right, open-hand check.
3. Check your opponent's wrist and simultaneously strike to the face with a right, open backhand.
4. Without recoiling the weapon, shift your weight, drop slightly and execute a downward palm strike to the midsection.
5. As the opponent's head drops, reposition yourself and raise him up with a right, rising forearm strike to the face.
6. Torque with a strong pivot right and hit him in the face with a left forearm strike.

EXAMPLE #2

1. Get in a left-foot-forward, on-guard stance and face your opponent.

2. Shift left to the outside and simultaneously parry your opponent's right punch. Throw a counter strike to his midsection with your right hand.

3. As opponent leans forward, his head will be near your shoulder.

4. Strike him with the shoulder, and this will mathematically reposition him upright.

5. Follow with a left forearm across the face.

6. End with a pivot left into the opponent to deliver a right punch to the midsection.

EXAMPLE #3

1. Assume a right-foot-forward on-guard stance and face the opponent.

2. Parry the opponent's left punch with a left, hand-open check.

3. Hit your opponent with a right foreknuckle punch.

4. Immediately follow-up with a palm strike to the abdomen with the same hand. Put some speed and body weight into the strike.

5. Torque to the left and hit your opponent in the face with a right elbow.

6. Finish with a sharp pivot to the right and throw a left ridgehand to the head.

FIGHTING PRINCIPLES

EXAMPLE #4

1. While you're standing at ease, your opponent grabs your lapel with his right hand.

2. Secure your opponent's right hand with your left hand as you shift left to widen your stance and prepare to throw a strike with your right hand.

3. Hit your opponent on the right side of his neck with a thrusting right hand strike.

4. While maintaining a grip on his wrist, follow-up with a right forearm smash downward onto your opponent's biceps.

5, 6. Release your grip on your opponent's wrist as you torque left for an elbow smash to his head. 7. Double tap with an immediate downward breaking, palm strike to your opponent's lead leg.

TORQUING: There are several types of torque. There is body torque that uses the hips, there is punching torque that uses the body and fist, and there is a reverse punch torque and wrist torque.

Torque relies on the snapping and whipping of the weapon or entire body at the correct time, distance, speed and power. Sometimes, you use the foundation of the ground for leverage. When you use the ground, you are not anchored, but you use its leverage to produce either a short whipping torque or a long whipping torque with your weapon. Furthermore, in the world of martial arts, most practitioners torque only on a horizontal plane, as in left to right, or visa versa. However, in fighting, torquing is also done on a vertical plane, as in up and down.

EXAMPLE #1

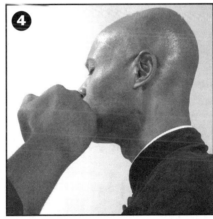

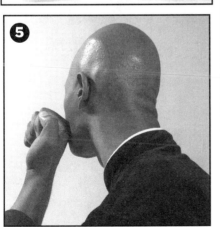

1. Assume a left on-guard stance and face your opponent.
2. Parry your opponent's left punch with your right hand and simultaneously strike with a left knifehand strike to the side of his head.
3. Using some wrist torque, execute a right hammer fist strike to your opponent's face.
4, 5. Close-up of torque in action.
6. Pivot right and finish with a short, left reverse punch to the chest.

EXAMPLE #2

1. Face your opponent and assume a left on-guard stance.
2. Side step to the left to avoid the opponent's attack as you parry his strike with both hands.
3. Pivot left into the opponent with a right forearm strike to the mid-section. This should force him to bend forward.
4. Pivot right for a downward forearm strike to the back of the neck.

EXAMPLE #3

1. Get in a neutral stance and face your opponent.
2. When your opponent throws a left punch to the midsection, shift to the right and check the blow with an open right-hand check.
3. Pivot right and shoot a thrusting finger strike to his eyes.
4. With a strong torque, pivot into a left palm strike to the midsection.
5. Immediately follow-up with a smashing left forearm strike to the face.
6. Pivot left and throw a right punch to the midsection.

EXAMPLE #4

1. Face your opponent and get in a neutral stance.

2. As the opponent throws a right punch to your stomach, side step to the left and hit his lead thigh with a crippling downward right punch.

3. Pivot left, torque and apply a wrenching two-hand armbar.

4. Follow-up with a right forearm smash to his lower ribs and stomach.

5. Pivot left and finish with a downward hammerfist strike to the back of your opponent's neck.

WALKING ON THE OPPONENT: This means you are in a continuous state of forward aggression. Most people, when they are hit, are instinctively going to take a step back. Walking on the opponent simply means you are going to advance in concert with the opponent as he is in retreat. It also means initially pressing the opponent into retreating at the same time and at the same pace that you are advancing with the attack. In this mode of attack, you step forward as if walking, with one foot following the other.

HIDDEN MOVES: As the name implies, these are movements sandwiched within a technique that an opponent cannot easily detect. These moves could be hidden because the field of vision of the opponent is obstructed or they can be disguised in subtle, yet devastating angles. With hidden moves, you place the opponent in a position to obtain a target of opportunity. Every movement creates an opportunity from which you can create another movement, etc. There is never *not* a target to hit and destroy.

FIGHTING PRINCIPLES

EXAMPLE A

1. This example of a hidden move takes advantage of the split second of time as the opponent is being struck in the face.

2. The temporary loss of vision gives a split-second window of opportunity for a left vertical punch to the ribs.

EXAMPLE B

1. Face your opponent with your right foot forward.
2. When your opponent throws a left palm strike to your face, parry at his elbow with your right hand.
3. A hidden move is applied by firing a quick right punch to the ribs. This is thrown under his extended left hand.

The following are specific drills that you, the fighter, can perform to develop your hidden moves. Read through the following material carefully and visualize the movements before you attempt to practice them.

DRILL 1

1. You and your partner should assume a fighting stance with your right foot forward.
2. Have your partner throw a right punch to your chest. Simultaneously check the strike with your left hand and shoot a vertical punch with your right hand. Step forward with your right foot on the movement. It's important to observe the sound the three movements make. The sound of your left hand check, your right vertical punch and your short step forward should be as one.
3. Your partner checks your vertical fist.
4. Shoot a quick left hand punch over the checked hand. When you connect, torque your body into the punch.

DRILL 2

This is a hand check, over-under drill that is a staple BKF drill. Although it is 20 years old, it remains effective as a basic drill and is still taught in schools today. Following are a few keys to remember as you perform this drill: put your body behind the strike, keep your body on-line, do not allow your opponent to disengage and stay with his backward movement.

1. From a fighting stance with your right foot forward, face your partner, who is in an on-guard stance, right foot forward.
2. Execute a right hand check and grab his lead hand while executing a left vertical punch to his chest (over his hand).
3. Step forward with your left foot and strike under his hand with a right punch to the stomach.

DRILL 3

1. Face your partner, and make sure your right foot is forward to his right foot forward on-guard stance.
2. Execute a right hand check of his lead hand as you throw a left punch to his chest.
3. As your partner ckecks this, step to the left and strike with a right ridge hand across his torso. You want to induce your partner to block this.
4. Snap a quick left punch to his face. This is the hidden move.
5. From this close range, you could also knee the opponent in the thigh. This is also a hidden move.

BONE-ON-BONE STRIKING: Actual combat has proven that one of the most devastating principles, both physically and psychologically, is the pain and trauma that results from a bone-on-bone technique. A bone-on-bone strike with the knuckle to your opponent's forehead will almost always result in a tearing of the skin and blood loss. Physically, the damage is not severe. However, the psychological effect can be. When a fighter sees his blood flowing freely, that could have an enormous impact on the fight.

With this in mind, a warrior should strategically prepare himself mentally. Visualize. Meditate. Train your mind and body so that it can be calmed and brought under control if you encounter a life-threatening situation or sustain blood loss from an injury.

EXAMPLE 1

Striking the sternum (Figures 1 and 2)

EXAMPLE 2

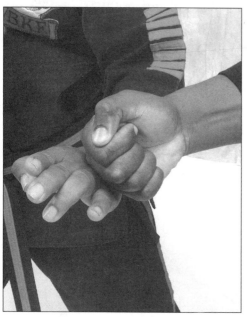

Striking the back of the hand

EXAMPLE 3

Striking the shins

EXAMPLE 4

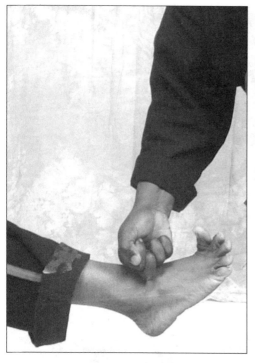

Striking the instep

EXAMPLE 5

Striking the knee

EXAMPLE 6

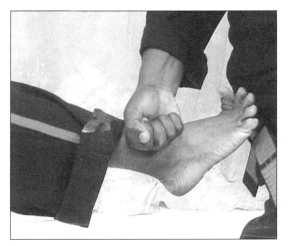

Striking above the ankle

EXAMPLE 7

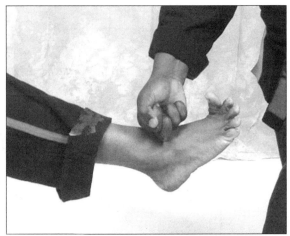

Knuckle strike to the instep

CRITICAL DISTANCE FIGHTING: The critical zone of combat is two feet away from the opponent. You should be capable of hitting the opponent with either hand from the head to the groin in a fraction of a second. Many skilled fighters reduce this distance to one foot. *(Example 1)*. Beyond two feet, a fighter moves out of range to properly execute certain techniques such as hand strikes. At this distance, kicking techniques would be applied *(Example 2)*. Moving away from this distance, the fighter moves into a safety zone *(Example 3)*.

EXAMPLE 1 (Distance)

EXAMPLE 2 (Distance)

EXAMPLE 3 (Distance)

HITTING THE OPPONENT OFF THE MARK: This deals with distance. You have to be at a distance in which you can touch or hit your opponent with either hand without moving your feet. With a lead hand punch, you should only have to lean forward slightly to be able to touch your opponent. With a rear hand punch, you have to shift your body forward without moving your feet. At the point of impact, push off your back leg. The "mark" is the distance between you and your opponent. The average fighter maintains a distance of about one foot, regardless of your height.

The following is a drill to build speed and the ability to hit the opponent off the mark. Again, as with the previous drills, visualize these movements before you practice them.

• Position yourself one foot away from your training partner with your left foot forward. The first movement that you make will be a left hand check (tap your partner's lead hand with your lead hand).

• Immediately follow-up with a right hand reverse punch to the chest without moving your feet until the point of impact.

• At the point of impact, step forward with your right foot and follow through with a left hand reverse punch to the chest.

• Do three sets of 15 repetitions for both sides. Try to increase your speed, awareness, power and timing gradually as you work each set.

BUILDING MOMENTUM ON THE ATTACK: You can practice this by tapping the lead hand of your opponent. Without moving your body or your feet forward, tap your opponent's lead hand once, twice or more. Then, follow-up with a strike. You may start slow, tapping the hand and perhaps throwing a light kick. You can slow yourself down or build yourself up, whichever you choose to do.

There are other ways to build momentum. When facing numerous matches in competition, gradually regulate your fighting momentum over the course of the event. When you engage in your first match, your momentum lags a bit. In this instance, you may start off with a kick or possibly checking the opponent's lead hand and follow up with a light punch. As you advance throughout the event, you should build momentum. Even if your opponent is using the same strategy, it does not matter. You still build your momentum. Keep in mind, however, that the same strategy that you are planning to use on the opponent, the opponent could also use on you. The opponent could be probing your reaction with exploratory moves like tapping your lead hand, for example. As you build your momentum, you should try to beat the opponent to the punch.

KEY THOUGHT: Your actions have a corresponding sound, such as the sound of your hand tapping against the opponent's hand. There is also the sound of the exchange of strikes. As momentum builds between you and your opponent, those "sounds" can actually help you to increase your speed if you pay attention to them, work with and manipulate their rhythms.

TOURNAMENT FIGHTING TIP: Most tournament fighters fight the same way continuously in each and every match. They never build momentum. Their actions are predictable and boring because they may advance with a quick move, but that momentum never changes. When a fighter begins to fight, he is not going to be at his maximum fighting speed. It does not matter if he loosens up or warms up. He should start off slowly and build his momentum as he goes.

Suppose you are looking to fight three matches. On your first match, try to keep the opponent from scoring while you attempt to score. However, you should not expect to be as sharp in your first match as you will be in your third. Remember, your momentum is supposed to build. After about three fights, you should be at the peak of your momentum and it should not decrease.

MARTIAL ARTS, MUSIC AND MATH

Rhythmical variations are mathematical and logical sequences. The rhythms that are considered "hip" are mathematically more sophisticated. In 1964, when a young Muhammad Ali, known then as Cassius Clay, won the world heavyweight title from Sonny Liston, Motown Records' "*The Sound of Young America*" was in full swing, breaking new ground with a dynamic new sound. Ali grew up listening to popular music's 4-4 rhythm patterns and not to the slower rhythms of the era before him.

In jazz, legends such as Charlie "Bird" Parker expressed the faster rhythms of bebop. Saxophone master John Coltrane moved the pace forward with 16-note patterns and so on. In the African-American community, where rhythm patterns change continuously, understanding musical concepts may help to increase your awareness, selection and use of rhythm patterns and thereby increase your ability to develop a more sophisticated physical vocabulary.

BASE RHYTHMS: These are rhythms that are at the bottom or base of an arrangement. In fighting, base rhythms give you a foundation, a beat. How a fighter can manipulate base rhythms can be extrapolated from these two classical examples: In European orchestral compositions, there is predominantly one rhythm pattern. There may be hundreds of instruments in the orchestra, but they are all playing on one base rhythm. Although most compositions are very melodic, you could say they are "mono-rhythmic." In a jazz ensemble, after establishing a base rhythm with as little as two instruments, players can vary the rhythm patterns to achieve a wider variety of musical patterns. In rap and hip hop, artists tend to stack voice and instrument rhythms on top of a base rhythm for more dynamic sounds and patterns.

STACKED RHYTHMS: The modern way of stacking rhythms actually goes back to Africa and the use of the drum. One drummer kept one beat while a second drummer played a counter beat over the first. To illustrate this, some music rhythms tend to be like waltzes with a 1-2-3, 1-2-3 pattern. The stacking is orderly and predictable.

As applied to fighting, the more you are able to stack rhythms and "vary" them, the more unpredictable you become. To illustrate this principle in physical terms, take basketball great Michael Jordan. What he and more advanced players have done is learned to stack rhythms. Their bodies may have a rhythm pattern going in one direction while their head and arms are going in another. They easily baffle the opposition, who often cannot decide on the correct counter move. The stacking of rhythm makes an attack more sophisticated. Fighters gain this through experience.

VARIATIONS ON A THEME: In using this principle, a warrior creates a theme or a pattern of movement and then destroys this pattern doing something completely different with it. For example, master Steve Muhammad has nine techniques that he pulls from, but he will also create and adapt those nine techniques to create thousands of different movements from just those nine. In his "Dance of Death" video, for example, Muhammad visualizes fighting nine people. He performs a kata, which not only promotes energy and stamina, but builds fighting spirit and the ability to create variations on a theme.

RHYTHMIC DISPLACEMENT: This term describes rhythm patterns that are displaced or off track. For example, you will find music that arrives on beats of 1, 2, 3, 4. With most standard music, the arrangements come in on a set pattern and beat. Whereas jazz music often comes in "ahead" of the beat or "behind" the beat. You hear it as, "AND" 1, "AND" 2, "AND" 3. The rhythm is off the beat. Of course, to know one is off the beat, one must know where the beat "is." The more dynamic rhythms tend to be displaced rhythms. They tend to be unpredictable.

AND FINALLY

A final word on music and rhythms. Although this concept may sound new to you, a lot of the same rhythmic patterns that work in music also work in martial arts and even in ordinary day to-day living. To assist you in appreciating this, we recommend you learn to play a musical instrument.

As a warrior, this is one way to properly train your nervous system. If a fighter has an "on the beat" nervous system, which you can see when that person walks, you can reasonably predict what response their nervous system is capable of giving in a fighting environment. A person's nervous system can be trained to achieve higher rhythmic states when one plays music, dances or engages in any musical activity. He would simply have more rhythmic options available.

GLOSSARY OF TERMS

BRIDGING THE GAP: Before striking, you must close and link the distance gap between you and your opponent. In the BKF, this is also known as striking from A to C.

CENTERLINE PRINCIPLE: This is an imaginary vertical line from the head to the toes that divides the body in half. You must simultaneously defend your line and attack your opponent's at all times during combat. This line is important because 90 percent of the nerve points that are vital to the human body and can end a confrontation, or lead to an end, are on this line. Also, by referencing the offensive and defensive techniques to the centerline, you create a stronger structural base for your movement.

Understanding this principle, in conjunction with limb rotation, allows each limb to act independently of the others while keeping the body in such a position that you can touch your opponent with either hand or foot at any time.

This is a simple principle but one of the most important ones of this system. The efficiency of trapping, hand flurries and economy of motion rely on this principle to a great extent. Breaking the centerline weakens the fighter's versatility.

Instead of using all weapons independently of one another, you should have them work together as a team. This allows for a much wider range of effective inside techniques, because both hands and feet can function offensively, defensively or both. Maintaining your centerline coverage gives you the opportunity to perform double-hand techniques. This greatly restricts the opponent's offensive potential. Keeping the centerline constant also allows you maximum use of your energy since it is flowing directly through your opponent.

The centerline is also used as a sight, the same way that a sight on a pistol is used. You use the centerline as a guide for striking the opponent.

CENTERLINE TRACKING: Your block/check redirects your opponent's weapons by moving along the centerline or parallel to it.

CONVERGING ENERGY: This principle refers to the power gained by moving the body forward through the opponent. In the BKF, power is developed by the sudden extension of the rear leg while delivering a weapon. Therefore, the leg must be put in a position that allows the extension toward the opponent. The torque of the body is used to set up the body and the rear leg.

ECONOMY OF MOTION: Using the smallest and most direct movements that are logically possible to hit or stop the opponent from hitting. For example, launching the reverse punch from the solar plexus instead of from the hip reduces the distance between the point of origin to the target, therefore being more economical.

ELBOW POCKET: Placing your elbow three inches in front of your body and angled toward your centerline provides the best positioning to attain maximum strength and flexibility for the six hand actions. To make sure you have the proper positioning, hold your other hand perpendicular to your solar plexus. Then, place your elbow next to your hand. That is the three inches you need. The hand and forearm can move in any direction, but the elbow never moves. Also, the hand and forearm should never pass the imaginary perpendicular line that creates the inner parameter, which intersects the elbow. If the arm is pressed too hard, it is better to give way with the whole body than to give way with the elbow, or violate that boundary line.

FOCUS: This refers to the withdrawal or recoil of a weapon faster than the extension at the moment of impact. By recoiling the weapon faster than it is extended, a sharp shock is applied to the target. It reduces the opponent's ability to roll or ride the blow to reduce the impact. This type of weapon delivery is ideally suited for bone-on-bone striking.

HAND ROTATION: To deliver multiple strikes alternating from the left hand to the right and vice versa, or from hand to leg.

INDEPENDENT UNIT MOVEMENT: A good fighter should have the ability to generate destructive power without making his body rigid or becoming one with the ground. Traditional martial arts teach that maximum power can only be achieved if the students anchor themselves to the ground and the entire body becomes rigid for a fraction of a second. The BKF does not teach this. Instead, we teach that mass times speed equals power. The mass is the entire body. How fast you can get the entire body to move is the speed. At the moment of impact, the weapon must be recoiled faster than it was extended. To create a situation that forces you to solidify yourself to the ground would break the continuity of motion and actually tend to slow you down. Remember that the power in karate comes from moving a small object quickly.

LEAD WEAPON: An attack with a lead weapon must fulfill the following criteria. First, it must be with a movement that allows you to cover ground quickly enough to beat your opponent's reactions. Second, the movement should be placed on the centerline between you and the opponent. Third, a good lead weapon attack should create the next opening for a follow-up.

MONITORING: While you are engaged in combat, you need a method of spotting the openings or the anticipated openings as soon as possible. This can be done by watching your opponent's hands or elbows. Watching with peripheral vision can give you the perceptual lead you need to apply whatever technique that best fits the situation.

POINT OF ORIGIN/NON-TELEGRAPHIC MOVEMENT: Moving the weapon and/or the body only in the desired direction.

SIX HAND ACTIONS

The six hand actions are used to move from a disadvantageous position to an advantageous position while fighting. They may be used singularly, but they are most often used in combination. Following are the six hand actions:

1. Pursue when withdrawn
2. Roll to deflect
3. Trap to immobilize
4. Receive to detain
5. Straight to penetrate
6. Disengage when pressed

SIMULTANEOUS ATTACK AND DEFENSE: To block, check or evade but strike the opponent at the exact same time.

SLOW FIGHTING: The importance of slow fighting is so great that it cannot be stressed enough. Slow fighting with a cooperative partner will help you learn the body's vocabulary, which will help to develop brain sight.

SPRING LOADING: While in a fighting stance, force your knees apart so that you create spring in your stance that can be used to aid your offensive or defensive footwork. While in this stance, you should be able to break into a full sprint at any time.

THEORY OF FACING: While you are in a fighting stance and maintaining centerline coverage, your body is positioned so that you are side facing or half-front facing. By taking one of these positions, you will present a smaller target to the opponent. Presenting a smaller target forces your opponent to be more accurate in the delivery of his weapons, at the same time reducing the area that you must protect. With your target centerline rotated away from the opponent, he is forced to use more complicated or sophisticated techniques to end the confrontation. They become exposed sooner and reveal an opportunity for you to end the confrontation.

WEAPON ALIGNMENT: At the moment of impact, the bones of the human body must be positioned so that the energy of the strike is transferred to the opponent in a clean and uninterrupted path.

WEAPON POSITIONING: This is a method of holding your weapons so that you will not have to reposition them before you strike. Your fists should be directed or pointed at your opponent. Your lead knee should be positioned so that it occupies the centerline as a kick is being delivered.

CHAPTER 7

BKF KENPO PHILOSOPHY

Skill in punching and kicking is only one

facet of the total man or the total woman.

Therefore, Advanced Strategic Principle No. 7 is ...

Seek balance.

The philosophy of BKF kenpo has been developed from more than 30 years of combined experience and teaching by grandmaster Steve Muhammad and Bishop Donnie Williams. Their philosophy, which is built upon the wisdom of ancient masters, is also based upon their lifetime of training and teaching. Combined, these have enabled them and their students to become highly effective fighters, world champions, and successful men and women in all walks of life.

They have recorded many of the BKF kenpo's insights and philosophy in their book "*The God Side of Kenpo*." Steve Muhammad, who embraces the Islamic tradition, and Donnie Williams, who embraces the Christian tradition, have both rediscovered the fact that the martial arts were built upon a foundation of spiritual discipline. Just as past martial arts masters such as Masutatsu Oyama, Morehei Ueshiba, Ed Parker, or even further back in history to the Kemetic Dynasties with Princes Baqet, Khety and Amenemha, or modern day masters such as Byong Yu, Steve Muhammad, Tadashi Yamashita, Greg McNeil and Donnie Williams, you will find that it has been their spiritual qualities that has set them apart and earned them the profound title of "Master." This title carried a lot of weight because these individuals became masters of themselves *(Figure A)*.

We cannot overly stress the fact that fighting alone is not the key to mastery through the martial arts. Fighting alone could not have enabled a great warrior and master strategist such as Nelson Mandela to achieve the success he has achieved for himself and his nation *(Figure B)*.

The failure to understand the need for balance is where many former BKF champions fell short in the past. Some highly skilled and talented warriors actually lost their lives due to their inability to recognize that there was more to the martial arts than being able to fight well. What they refused to understand was that there must be a mental, physical and spiritual balance in all things. Therefore, in your daily training, as you strive for excellence and map out your strategy for success, you should keep these thoughts in mind.

The Spirit of God-like thinking, this is what brings about balance.
If the martial art that you are practicing does not lead to God's thinking,
if it does not bring about balance.
Then, something is wrong with it.
Throw it out.

Nothing in existence is greater than what you have in your mind.
We have got to understand that, like a drop of water in the ocean,
the mind is an ocean.

୧୭

The art of war relies on knowledge. Knowledge is the key.
The warrior must have knowledge of tactics, which represent
the physical applications,
strategy, which represent the mental applications,
and knowledge of planning,
which comes from consistent practice.

୧୭

Feigning is an art. It is the key to being a successful warrior/fighter.
Feigning enhances mathematical, rhythmic motion while fighting.
All great warriors had feigns and jerks in their fighting.
Feigning speeds up the reaction process of the brain,
both in offense and defensive movements.

୧୭

The warrior knows and studies himself.

୧୭

If you do not reject wisdom, wisdom will not reject you.

*The mind and body as one should fight with maximum ease
and relaxation.
When the mind and body become one, it fights with maximum ease
and relaxation.
If you hurry, the mind and body will not become one.*

Use your energy strongly to watch intently over your mind.

ભ

*Emptiness of the mind will give the brain a chance for
high speed thought.
High speed thought can be called adaptability.
High speed thought is what you have learned, which is fluidity
of mind.*

ભ

*In fighting, you have to be aware of what went before and
what comes after.*

ભ

*In dealing with an enemy,
know that a people who cannot protect what they develop
will always be oppressed.*

ભ

*We must stop being victims of aggression.
Know your enemy, respect your enemy.
Don't fear your enemy, and by no means,
do you love your enemy.
Survival is a key element for human growth.
Cooperation and balance are keys for success.*

Figure A - Masters of the martial arts such as Byong Yu (from left to right) Steve Muhammad, Tadashi Yamashita, Dr. Stanford McNeil and Donnie Williams develop mastery over self and understand their world by understanding themselves.

Photo by Mark Campbell

In fighting a powerful opponent,
you should know that you don't attack.
You induce that opponent to come out of his
stronghold.
Sometimes you do this by showing weakness.

It is critical that we understand that
people without a mental, physical and spiritual defense system
are a people without a future
or a people at the mercy of the enemy.

ള♂

The modest person is strong
and for one who is true in word and just in deed,
houses are opened to the humble
and a wide seat is given to the one who is gentle in speech
and conduct.
But sharp knives stand ready for the unrighteous,
for there is no entrance except for the righteous.

ള♂

In training to fight a powerful opponent,
train and learn to live well under duress,
and to survive chaos.

ള♂

There is an art to the knowledge of how to take advantage
of an opponent.

Warriors should be skilled in speech so that they will succeed.
The tongue of a man is his sword,
and effective speech is stronger than all fighting.
None can overcome this skill.

ೞ

In training, train to develop strength so that you are not easily
affected or upset.
Train to have strength so that you are morally powerful,
having strength of character and will.
Train to have special competency or ability.
Train to have strength intellectually, to be able to think
vigorously and clearly.
Train to have strength in governing or leading with firm, right-
eous authority.
Train to have strength so that you are not easily defeated.
Train to be able to resist or endure attacks.

ೞ

In training, train to develop respectability.
Train to be worthy of respect.
Train to develop excellence and good quality.
Train to have a respectable reputation.
Respectfully is the way you live and behave.

Figure B - In 1999, three generations of righteous African warriors were represented in this historic meeting in South Africa between Nelson Mandela, Wesley Snipes and grandmaster Steve Muhammad.   *Courtesy of SMCM Enterprises*

STEVE MUHAMMAD QUOTES ON BRUCE LEE

"I was fighting in a tournament and that year, for whatever reason, I was on that year. After the match, this guy walked up to me and lightly tapped me on the shoulder, so I turned around. He said, "You have extremely fast hands." So I replied, "Thank you." Then he turned to walk away but stopped and turned back around to me and asked, "You know me?" I replied, "No sir." Then he quietly said "Bruce. Bruce Lee" and turned again to walk away. I shouted "Ooh!" and jumped to embrace him. He looked different than when I saw him in the *"Green Hornet,"* so I didn't recognize him until he said his name."

"While Bruce studied me for speed, Ed Parker gave him something different. He had timing which will equal speed if you have timing. Bruce in fact wasn't that fast, but he had what you would call "uncanny timing" which made him seem much faster. It *made* him much faster than the people who didn't have timing."

"Bruce had a saying that I live by today. He said, 'Be composed, but don't stand still. Be mobile, but don't move. Don't attack, strike. Hit your opponent on his first move. Move only to counter or attack.'"

"You are mobile in mind. You don't have to be mobile in body. You can't put your mind in neutral and expect to be able to move like you do a car. And this is

Sculpture of Bruce Lee by Nijel Binns, BPG.

Courtesy of Nijart International

what he was speaking of. You can be stationary but not set because the body has to be ready to shift and move in whatever direction you want it to go. You don't have to be mobile and dance around and shift to be able to move when it is time to move on your opponent. That is what he was talking about."

"Understand the meaning of this Bruce Lee riddle and you will also understand Brain Sight and subconscious fighting."

"No one has studied Bruce Lee. They have studied the movements but no one has studied Bruce Lee. In that saying he told you what he was growing into. He had not gotten there yet but he was growing into it. Nobody could be Bruce Lee. When Bruce Lee died, he took Bruce Lee and his style with him. He never got around to presenting the style to anyone else who can repeat it in the manner in which he created it. He died too soon. I think the key is in that statement."

"You can tell by the language Bruce used that he was still growing and would grow the rest of his life. He had what you call "weak side/strong side." In the art of fighting, as you grow older, you eliminate weak side/strong side, and you just become a fighter."

"Once you get to a certain level, you can actually break his words down and understand the direction in which he was going."

Sculpture of Steve Muhammad
by Edward Muhammad
Courtesy of Nijart International

A FINAL NOTE ON BECOMING
A SUCCESSFUL TOURNAMENT COMPETITOR

As time moves on, advances in technology will influence every new generation of martial artist and competitor. However, while new training methods, more efficient techniques and better safety gear often improve the physical abilities of an athlete, the key to truly becoming a great warrior and successful competitor lies in one thing ... attitude.

Great fighters such as Steve Muhammad and Donnie Williams have achieved lasting success both in and out of the ring, because of their sportsmanship and proper conduct as competitors. What makes their achievements highly significant is that they were able to reach these levels of success despite of the often blatant displays of racism that they faced in their era. While the modern competitor may also face these obstacles in modern times, Steve Muhammad and Donnie Williams discovered that if they remained clear in their commitment to uplift their students and remained united behind a code of conduct that is befitting of a true warrior, it would enable them to overcome every obstacle.

One principle that you can surely adhere to that will assist you in becoming great and finding success in the world of tournament fighting, as well as in the daily arena of life is simply this:

Remain respectful to yourself and to your opponent.